TRANSFORMATION

Transformation: The Journey from Breakdown to Breakthrough

Print ISBN: 978-1-971052-11-3

Ask & It Is Written Publishing House
www.AskandItIsWritten.com

TRANSFORMATION

THE JOURNEY FROM BREAKDOWN TO BREAKTHROUGH

COMPILED BY ELIAS PATRAS

FOREWORD

BY ELIAS PATRAS

There are moments in life that invite us inward, and there are moments that change us forever.

Going Within to Heal, the first book in **The Within Series**, opened the door to the courage it takes to face what is wounded, tender, and unfinished within us. It reminded us that healing begins when we stop running from ourselves and start listening to what is asking to be seen, felt, and understood.

This second book, *Transformation: The Journey from Breakdown to Breakthrough*, carries that journey forward.

Because going within is not the end of the story. It is the beginning.

Once we begin to heal, something starts to shift. The patterns we lived by no longer fit the person we are becoming. The pain we once avoided begins to reveal its lessons. The breakdowns we feared or resisted can become the very places where truth rises, strength is rebuilt, and breakthrough begins.

This book is a collection of stories from people who have walked through difficult seasons of life and discovered something meaningful on the other side. Not because the road was easy. Not because they had every answer. But because something within them kept calling them forward, even in the middle of uncertainty, loss, grief, change, or unraveling.

Transformation rarely arrives in neat, polished steps. It often meets us in the messy middle. In the questions. In the tears. In the surrender. In the moments we realize that what once protected us may now be the very thing keeping us stuck. And in the quiet courage it takes to begin again.

Each story in these pages offers its own kind of wisdom. Some may feel familiar, as if they are echoing your own life. Others may stretch your heart and deepen your compassion. Together, they remind us that breakdown does not mean failure. Sometimes it is the moment life strips away what is no longer true, so something deeper, stronger, and more honest can rise.

That is the spirit of this book, and of **The Within Series** itself.

While each book stands on its own, together they reflect a deeper path: going within, moving through transformation, and rising into the freedom of becoming limitless and free. This book meets us in the middle of that journey, in the raw and sacred space where life has broken something open, and something new is trying to emerge.

My hope is that as you move through these stories, you feel seen. I hope you feel less alone in your own hard moments. I hope you are reminded that even when life feels uncertain or undone, there can still be meaning, healing, and growth. And most of all, I hope you remember this: breakdown is not the whole story.

Breakthrough is possible.

In honor of your journey within,

Elias

A special thanks to Maria Bennett for her assistance with this book.

CONTENTS

CHAPTER 1

Pulmonary Awakening

by Maria Bennett

Maria Bennett

Maria Bennett lives on California's Central Coast, where she and her husband tend a small farm with chickens, four dogs, and four cats. A mother of three compassionate adult children, she draws inspiration from family, animals, and the quiet rhythms of rural life. Her writing explores resilience, humor, and the extraordinary hidden in ordinary moments. When she's not writing, she's caring for her farm, observing life's small miracles, and reflecting on the stories that connect us all. Learn more at www.harmonyhouseranch.com.

PULMONARY AWAKENING

BY MARIA BENNETT

I was wrapping up my first year as an Administrative Assistant to the Principal at our local high school when everything started shifting again. The district was reorganizing, and my supervisor, the principal, had just been told he was being demoted. The whole building felt on edge, as if everyone were waiting for something to explode. His behavior became unpredictable, and I found myself trying to keep the school running smoothly while he unraveled. My days stretched into twelve-hour marathons, fueled by coffee and whatever adrenaline I had left.

I was also carrying more weight than my body could comfortably handle, and the job had me sitting most of the day. My joints ached, my energy was low, and every step felt like I was dragging myself through mud. For four months, I pushed through the stress, the exhaustion, and the physical strain. When he finally left, and our assistant principal stepped into the role, the campus seemed to exhale. I told myself I could exhale, too, but deep down, something in my body was already whispering that things were not okay.

Summer arrived, and the pace relaxed. A sense of calm pervaded the building. The hallways were still, dust motes drifting in the sunbeams that fell through high windows. It was just me, the new principal, and a couple of others preparing for the coming year. I'd been having dizzy spells off and on for about six months. They usually struck when I got up too quickly or moved suddenly. I shrugged them off. I'd always had a low resting heart rate, and even at its highest, my blood pressure rarely rose above 120 over 80. Getting 'the spins' when standing too fast had been happening since I was a teenager.

Sometimes I'd wake in the middle of the night dizzy, the room tipping and swirling in the dark. I'd go downstairs and sit in the easy chair with my feet raised, waiting for it to pass. It always did—until it didn't.

It was the last Saturday in July. I woke early, already dizzy. The ceiling seemed to sway slightly as if the whole room were breathing. I went downstairs to ride it out in the chair, but this time, nothing worked. The room kept spinning, the walls pulsing in and out. I moved to the wall and slid down to the floor, sitting with my back against the wall, waiting for the world to steady. It didn't.

My husband came downstairs, took one look at me, and asked how I was feeling. His voice was tight with concern, the kind of calm that comes from suppressing panic. We talked briefly, and he said, "Let's go to the emergency room and get this checked out."

But I was not going to the ER in my pajamas. "Okay," I said, "but I'm changing into real clothes first."

Looking back, I marvel at my stubbornness. But at that moment, I was determined to maintain some sense of control. My husband followed me upstairs because I was still dizzy. About halfway up, the spinning intensified. I was afraid I might fall, so I hurried the rest of the way—big mistake.

At the top of the stairs, I couldn't breathe. It was as if someone had flipped a switch inside my chest and shut off the air. I was gasping, pulling in air, but getting nothing. My lungs seized, and panic clawed at the edges of my mind. Then everything slowed down, and out of nowhere, I heard a voice, clear as day, say, "This is what your dad felt."

Where did that come from? My father had died of lung cancer six years earlier, a victim of secondhand smoke. But right then, I was too focused on trying to breathe to think about it. If I survived, I told myself, I'd unpack that later. Panic was rising fast, cold and electric.

I stumbled to the side of the bed and managed to squeak out, “I can’t breathe!” I sat down, trying to remember the Johnson breathing technique I’d learned in childbirth classes. The Johnson method was designed to help control labor pains. I was hoping it would calm me. It didn’t. My body started convulsing, and I fell back onto the bed.

I remember my husband’s voice on the phone; steady, calm, precise, as he spoke to the 911 operator. I heard the sirens approaching, faint at first, then louder, until they filled the room. My vision tunneled. The world dimmed. Then everything went black.

The next thing I knew, EMTs were there, moving quickly and efficiently, placing an oxygen mask over my face. Cool air filled my lungs, sharp and metallic. They lifted me onto a stretcher and rushed me to the emergency room, lights flashing, sirens wailing; a wild symphony of urgency and survival.

That’s when it hit me how close to death I’d come. When the body shuts down, control of basic functions ceases. I had voided myself. Lying there in that hospital bed, the reality sank in: I had nearly died. After several scans and tests, the emergency room doctor told me that I had several blood clots in my lungs. He called it a pulmonary embolism, which is often fatal.

They admitted me to the ICU for observation. Everything that followed felt surreal, as if I were floating somewhere between waking and dreaming.

I was hooked up to heart monitors and oxygen, the steady beep of the machines reminding me I was still here. The smell of antiseptic filled the air, sharp and clean. At some point, I drifted off to sleep until my nurse shook me awake, her voice urgent. “Are you okay? Are you okay?”

I blinked, disoriented. “What? I was sleeping.”

She explained that my heart rate had slowed so much that it triggered the alarms. It happened twice that night, each time her voice pulling me back from the edge.

The next morning, they ran an EKG and several other tests. The room hummed with machines and quiet efficiency. When the tech left, my nurse came in and asked, "Are you an elite athlete?"

I looked at her, puzzled, then down at my very overweight body, then back up. "Do I look like an elite athlete?" I said.

We both burst out laughing, big, uncontrollable belly laughs with tears streaming down our faces. It was the first real laugh I'd had in months, and it felt like oxygen in a different way, pure, life-giving release.

She said, "Your heart is in great shape. The tech actually asked if you'd been an athlete."

I grinned. "The only elite thing I've done lately is eat too much of the wrong food."

At least I hadn't lost my sense of humor.

Three days later, they released me with blood-thinning medication and injections to help prevent more clots. The drive home felt strange, like the world was both brighter and more fragile. The sunlight looked sharper somehow, the air heavier and more precious.

Then came the judgments. My mother, my brother, my sister, my in-laws, my co-workers, some friends, everyone except my family and closest friends.

"You brought this on yourself."

"You need to lose weight."

"You've let yourself go."

"You're still fat. Why won't you do something about it?"

"Don't you realize how dangerous this was?"

It amazed me how people could say such things and then wrap their cruelty in a we care about you tone. Their words stung more than the IV needle. It dawned on me then that those comments weren't about concern at all; they were about them: their discomfort, their fear, their need to feel superior by cutting me down.

Judgment is not caring. Judgment is a mirror people hold up to make themselves feel better about what they see in someone else.

I had nearly died. I'd heard a voice, maybe my father's, or my own subconscious, reminding me how fragile this life is. A voice that brought clarity to what had happened. A voice that, to this day, I have no idea where it came from, but it's really not important where it came from. I'd felt the edge of that darkness, the quiet surrender that comes when the body gives up, and the spirit begins to let go.

And yet, I am still here.

Breathing.

Laughing.

Alive.

CHAPTER 2

Picking up the Pennies

by Mandy Covington

Mandy Covington

Mandy Covington is a writer whose work is rooted in resilience, truth, and the quiet power of survival. Born with a deep sensitivity to the world around her, Mandy has always found meaning in the small, overlooked details of life—moments most people pass by without noticing. Her writing reflects that same attentiveness, capturing the emotional undercurrents of hardship, hope, and the unexpected signs that guide us through our darkest chapters.

Mandy's journey has been shaped by experiences that tested her strength in ways few ever face. After enduring homelessness in Las Vegas, navigating daily danger, emotional suppression, and profound loss, she emerged with a story that demanded to be told. Her chapter "Picking Up the Pennies" stands as a testament not only to survival but to the mysterious ways life leaves breadcrumbs for us to follow when everything else falls apart.

Now living in Idaho, Mandy continues to rebuild her life with the same quiet determination that carried her through those thirty-two days. She writes with honesty, vulnerability, and a deep reverence for the small signs that helped her hold on. Her two oldest cats—her last remaining companions from that time—still walk beside her, reminders of both what she lost and what she saved.

Mandy's work invites readers to look closer, feel deeper, and recognize that hope doesn't always arrive loudly. Sometimes it appears as something as small as a penny, waiting quietly in our path.

PICKING UP THE PENNIES

BY MANDY COVINGTON

Las Vegas looks different when you're not there for the lights. When you're not a tourist, not a gambler, not someone chasing neon promises. When you're homeless, the city strips itself down to its bones. The glitter fades, and what's left is heat, noise, and a kind of loneliness that settles into your skin.

The first penny showed up on Boulder Highway, at the very beginning of everything falling apart. We were pushing a huge kennel with broken wheels—six animals total, five cats crammed inside, and the dog walking beside us—the whole thing rattling and dragging against the pavement. Cars roared past us, the heat rising off the asphalt in waves, and we had no idea where we were going. We were just moving because standing still felt even more dangerous.

The kennel kept catching on cracks in the sidewalk, jerking out of our hands, the wheels wobbling like they were about to snap off completely. The cats were crying, scared and confused, and every sound from them made my chest tighten. My partner was tense, angry, and overwhelmed, and I was trying to hold myself together because he didn't allow me to break down. Not even then. Not even with everything collapsing around us.

We were stranded on Boulder Highway with nowhere to go, no plan, no safety, and six terrified animals depending on us. My mind was spinning, my heart racing, and I remember thinking, How did we end up here? How do we survive this?

And then I saw it. A penny. Right there on the sidewalk, almost glowing in the sun.

It made no sense—in the middle of all that chaos, all that fear, all that noise—something so small and quiet was waiting for me. I bent down, picked it up, and for a moment, the world stopped spinning. It felt like the tiniest whisper cutting through the panic: You're not alone. Keep going.

I slipped it into my pocket without knowing it would be the first of thirty-two; without knowing that this tiny coin would become the one steady thing in a month where everything else was falling apart.

Every day in that Motel 6 felt like the same heavy loop. It wasn't one of the nice ones off the Strip—it was in one of the roughest parts of Vegas, the kind of place where you slept with one ear open and your shoes by the door. I stayed inside as much as I could. The room was small, but it was the only space where I felt even a little bit safe.

I didn't go out unless I had to. Walking the dog. Going next door to the 7-Eleven for something cheap to eat. Or heading to an appointment when I couldn't avoid it. That was my whole world. Four walls and the stretch of pavement between the motel and the convenience store. The days blurred together, each one a grind, each one a reminder of how far from home I felt.

And layered on top of the danger outside was the danger inside—the emotional pressure I lived under every minute. My partner didn't allow me to feel anything. If I cried, he snapped at me. Told me I was making things worse. Told me emotions were a weakness we couldn't afford. So I learned to swallow everything. To keep my face still. To hold my breath instead of letting the tears fall.

Every moment became a balancing act—trying to stay safe in a dangerous place while also trying not to upset the person who was supposed to protect me. His stress became my responsibility. His anger became another threat I had to navigate. His fear turned into pressure that sat on my chest day and night.

And in the middle of all that, the pennies kept showing up.

It didn't matter if I stepped out at dawn or late afternoon. It didn't matter if I was exhausted, angry, numb, or just going through the motions. Somewhere along my path—on the sidewalk, near the curb, by the stairs, in the dirt—there it would be. A small copper coin, waiting for me like it had been placed there on purpose.

I didn't just toss the pennies into my bag with everything else. They had their own place—a little pocket off to the side, a spot I never used for anything else. It became their home. Every time I slipped a new penny in there, I could feel the small weight of the others shifting, settling, almost like they were greeting the new arrival.

That pocket became sacred. I didn't keep food there, or receipts, or anything practical. Just the pennies. Just the proof that each day had given me something—a whisper, a reminder, a sign that I wasn't walking through that desert of uncertainty alone.

After a few days, I started to expect it. Then I started to look forward to it. It was strange, almost surreal—the way something so tiny could matter so much. But something inside me kept whispering that it did matter. That even the smallest things could carry meaning. That even the smallest signs could keep a person going.

And then came the losses—the ones that still ache when I think about them.

I lost three of my cats during that time, pieces of my heart I never got back. And I lost my dog too, the one who walked those scorching sidewalks with me, who stayed by my side through every lonely day in that Motel 6. Those losses still sit heavy in a place inside me that doesn't have words.

And then there was the loss that didn't come from death, but from desperation. My partner—my best friend at the time—reached a breaking point. We were both drowning, both scared, both pushed past what any person should have to endure. But he made a choice I couldn't stop. He committed a crime out of sheer desperation, and he was arrested.

It happened just a few days before I stepped onto the bus to come home. One moment he was beside me, trying to figure out the next step with me, and the next he was gone—swallowed by the system, leaving me standing alone in Las Vegas with nothing but my bag, my animals, and the crushing realization that I had to finish the rest of this nightmare by myself.

When I finally made it home to Idaho, I had only my two oldest cats left. Out of the six animals I started with, they were the only ones who survived that chapter with me.

It wasn't until a few weeks later, sitting alone in my room at the Extended Stay, that I finally counted the pennies. My bag was on the bed beside me, the same bag I'd carried through every one of those days in Las Vegas. I reached into the little pocket where I'd kept them—their pocket—and felt the familiar weight.

Curiosity nudged me. Or maybe it was something deeper. A need for confirmation of what I already knew.

I poured them out onto the bedspread. They rolled a little, catching the soft light of the room, each one a tiny echo of a day I had survived. I lined them up carefully, almost reverently.

When I finished counting, I just sat there, staring. Thirty-two. Exactly thirty-two pennies. One for every single day—from the day the court ordered the eviction to the day I stepped onto the bus to come home.

It hit me all at once. The timing. The precision. The quiet, steady presence of something watching over me when I felt most alone.

Those pennies weren't random. They weren't a coincidence. They were a calendar of survival. A breadcrumb trail. A quiet, persistent reminder that even in the hardest stretch of my life, I was never walking alone.

I gathered them back into their pocket, but this time with reverence. They weren't just pennies anymore. They were proof that I endured, that I was guided, that I was held through every single one of those thirty-two days.

I don't find pennies every day anymore. I don't need to. But when I do see one—on a sidewalk, in a parking lot, tucked in a corner where no one else would notice—I pick it up. I slip it into my pocket. And for a moment, I'm back in Las Vegas, walking through the heat, carrying grief I didn't yet understand, but still being guided forward.

And I remember: hope doesn't always arrive in grand gestures. Sometimes it shows up as a single penny, waiting quietly in your path.

CHAPTER 3

Country Strong

by Jessica Curran

Jessica Curran

Jessica Curran, born in West Monroe, Louisiana, and later moving to Glennville, Georgia at the age of 7, would never have imagined the significant losses ahead in her life before the young age of 34. With a master's in counseling, she became a high school counselor in Greenville, South Carolina, before moving to Roswell, Georgia, where her losses forced her to give up her career and become a stay-at-home mom, taking over the family business as a fourth-generation cricket farmer. She happily lives that role as a mother to three young children and a wife to her Australian-born-and-raised husband, Liam.

Jessica has endured her journey of grief and loss and knows it is a journey that never truly ends. But behind the door of her losses awaited transformation, and Jessica took the key, unlocked a life of fulfillment, and realized that grief and joy can coexist.

COUNTRY STRONG

BY JESSICA CURRAN

July 25, 2015, was the best day of my life—the day my husband, Liam, and I married in Savannah, Georgia. We stood before 150 family members and friends. They had traveled from around the world to celebrate with us. His family and friends flew in from Sydney, Australia. That week, we showed them my Southern roots in Savannah and in my hometown of Glennville, a town of about 5,000 residents in the middle of the country. They learned to shoot on our land using paper plate targets. They toured my "Bamaw's" 19th-century farmhouse and visited our family business—Armstrong's Cricket Farm. My great-grandfather founded it in 1947 to serve the local fishermen, and my dad, a third-generation cricket farmer, later ran it and began selling to reptile stores as well. After a bit of culture shock and some fun for the Aussies, we headed to the beach to tie the knot.

We married on a Saturday at Tybee Island Chapel, then danced and drank late into the night. Joyful newlyweds, sweaty in the southern humidity, we ran through sparklers to a waiting Rolls-Royce as the clock struck midnight. Fireworks lit up the night sky as I said a bittersweet goodbye to my maiden name, Armstrong, and unknowingly, the last time my full family and Liam's full family would ever be together.

After the best week of our lives—our honeymoon in Ocho Rios, Jamaica—change awaited me at home. I drove to Glennville to pick up our Boston Terrier, Khloe, who'd stayed at my dad's, her paradise for chasing squirrels. It was once my parents' house, but now belonged to just my dad. Though divorced after 30 years, he and my mom, Debbie, stayed close friends. They talked almost daily and spent a lot of time together. That night, my dad was relaxed, grilling for just the two of us. With the wedding payments and hosting behind him, he carried a lightness I wish had lasted. By morning, everything changed.

I woke in my childhood bed to a call from my older sister, Paige. She'd received texts: our cricket farm was on fire. I leapt up and drove five minutes up the road. The sight was unforgettable: our original 1950s building in flames, my dad and his employees staring in disbelief. Our small-town fire department could not save it. The building collapsed, killing six million crickets—a third of our inventory—and turning my dad's newfound peace to ashes.

Thankfully, the fire spared the family business, allowing operations to continue through rebuilding. But our challenges persisted. Less than two weeks later, my dad's father, Bill Armstrong, died after a long struggle with dementia. A World War II and Korean War Army pilot, he later ran our second Louisiana cricket farm and deeply shaped my dad's life. I watched my dad grieve while rebuilding the farm. In the hardest times, resilience and legacy intertwined—a lesson I would soon face myself.

Amid the hard times, we received good news—the birth of our first child, Brooklyn, on September 14, 2016. It was a day I will always remember with great pride and gratitude, arriving just four days shy of my dad's 60th birthday. Surrounded by my dad, my mom, my older siblings Paige and Jacob, my best friend Brooke, and Liam's mom Deborah, I felt fortunate to have my support system on this monumental day for our family. We were discharged, and within days of being home, we learned my dad had been quietly battling a months-long illness, first diagnosed as Lyme disease. But his health kept declining. Seeing him that day, we knew something was wrong. Two weeks after Brooklyn's birth, further testing revealed the devastating truth. My dad was dying of stage 4 cholangiocarcinoma, bile duct cancer. With this news, the hardest chapter of my life began—a life of grief I never could have imagined.

My dad fought cancer bravely, but it was found too late. While my parents and siblings slept in our childhood home, Dad quietly left us for his eternal home. He died on November 19, just seven weeks after his diagnosis and 18 months after his own dad. I was 29—still the baby of the family and a daddy's girl, something he never let me forget. Nothing prepares you to say goodbye to a parent. "It's okay to go. We'll be okay," I whispered, needing him to hear but only half believing it myself. I wasn't okay, and wouldn't be for a long time.

The day after he died, we learned my siblings and I would inherit the family business. This marked the start of another transition. I was a stay-at-home mom with no farm experience and had planned to return to my former career in school counseling. In the following months, Mom, my siblings, and I drove between Atlanta and Glennville. We learned to become business owners and packed our childhood home. Closing its doors for the last time felt like losing my past and the memories my parents built. Navigating this while grieving made it even harder. Between losing my dad, saying goodbye to our family home, and postpartum depression, I knew I could not handle it all. I admitted I needed help and reached out to a Christian therapist, seeing her weekly for many months. This was my first step toward healing.

The year that followed was filled with grief, but support from close friends and family softened the pain. Still, life took another turn for my older brother Jacob—a gentle, big-hearted class clown battling addiction and chronic heart and lung issues. He spent much of his adult life in and out of hospitals, rehab, or living with my mom in Jasper, Georgia. In January 2018, he was hospitalized for a severe airborne illness that damaged his lungs and required weeks of antibiotics. We visited often, bringing his favorite meals and gummy bears. He lit up when his nieces, Avery, Charlotte, or Brooklyn, visited. With just a week of treatment left, we began planning his discharge. He requested a fish fry and joked about a "welcome home parade." Days before he was to go home, scans revealed an enlarged heart, and he needed further testing. In our family group chat with my mom and sister, he sent a picture from the ambulance. We encouraged him to get out for a walk and enjoy the warm February day, but he replied he was too tired. It was an unusual response. An hour later, my mom called. "Jessie," she said, her voice shaking, "Jacob died."

This was a phone call I had feared for years, but now it was real. I was broken. Jacob was just 33. I ran to the sliding door and pleaded with the heavens, 'God, please don't take him! We can't lose anyone else.' But it was too late. Jacob died on February 27, 2018, 18 months after our dad died. The welcome-home parade he received was one only angels could attend. We were left with more flames turned to ashes, scattered through our lives.

My mom struggled deeply with losing her only son. The stress of losing Jacob and my dad, her high school sweetheart, was overwhelming. She suffered a stroke. Although she recovered physically, it changed her personality and deepened the depression she had lived quietly with. We began to miss our bubbly mom and 'Maw.' She was there, but rarely felt the same.

Yet again, with great sadness came great joy when I gave birth to Tristan, the first grandson on both sides of the family. Even during this difficult time, my mom adored baby Tristan. I know he reminded her of when Jacob was a baby. Over time, I saw that God gave me a child during each season of loss and grief. I believe He knew I needed them more than they needed me. My children are a blessing in this season. They are my reason for waking up and moving forward. In 2021, we completed our family with the birth of our third child, Declan. When my mom heard the news, she laughed and joked that she might have to move in to help raise three children under four. As a mom of three herself, if anyone could handle what lay ahead, it was her.

Mom began traveling with her childhood friend, Kendy, whom she had recently reconnected with. In April 2021, they were thrilled to visit the Blue Ridge Mountains in Tennessee and Dollywood.

She FaceTimed me from their cabin, bundled up in a white robe, to show me the stunning snowy mountains. The mountains were beautiful, and so was she, with the sunset glowing on her freshly cleansed face. I was solo parenting that weekend, and the kids needed me at the moment, so we said our goodbyes and hung up, planning to speak the next day about her Dollywood trip.

The following Sunday morning, while watching an online church service with my children, I got a call from Kendy.

"Hello?" I answered.

"Jessie," she said, her voice trembling, "something is wrong with your mom. She won't wake up."

For a moment, I felt as if I were dreaming. I asked Kendy questions; each answer made my heart sink. My children—then five, two, and nine months—looked at me with concern. They still needed me, even as my world tilted. Kendy called the paramedics while my sister and I stayed on the line from our homes in Georgia. We listened as they tried to revive her. Then, just like that, their efforts ended. My mom was gone.

Major flames. So many ashes. I was an orphan—an awful word that cuts deep at any age. At 34, I had lost my parents, my brother, and three grandparents—all within six years. Only my sister and I remained. I felt hopeless, and anxiety and depression stayed with me. Yet life pressed on.

Now I had a choice: sit with misery or reclaim my joy. I had every excuse for self-pity, but each day required a deliberate decision not to surrender. That was what my loved ones would have wanted and what my family needed from me.

I was undergoing a profound personal transformation in nearly every aspect of my life. When my children lost their grandparents in the States, I stepped into that absence—being both a steady presence and the fun, slightly crazy uncle they missed. Not wanting them to lose those relationships, I balanced spoiling them as my parents would while also being their mother.

I became a business owner, learning to shoulder the responsibility and legacy of a family farm begun four generations ago. Simultaneously, I deepened my relationship with God and sought clarity about Heaven and death. I found not fear, but beauty—a truth that gave me immeasurable peace.

Finally, I witnessed the quiet miracle of friends and neighbors becoming family. While I yearn for the holiday gatherings, birthday parties, lake days, and Sunday lunches I once shared, my closest friends stepped in with rescuing love, filling the empty spaces. The loss of my family altered my perspective in ways I never expected—an unexpected gift.

When people hear my story, they often ask how I manage to live a life of joy and fulfillment. I tell them it's because I still have so much to be grateful for—not only today, but also for what I had in my past. For example, I was blessed to have supportive parents who loved and nurtured me. Additionally, three of my grandparents lived until their late 80s, and I had a brother with whom I shared hilarious and precious memories. Now, I am happily married with three children, living in a community we love, and a sister and business partner who is my best friend. This is where I strive to keep my focus. Most importantly, my faith in God assures me I will see my loved ones again. That is the greatest gift of all.

I'm forever grateful I sought therapy for my grief and anxiety, especially EMDR's impact. Spiritual guidance from Elias Patras also helped me heal. He reminded me that love and connection endure beyond loss if we remain open to them.

My husband extended grace during my darkest days and is my rock. Meanwhile, my children, without knowing, have given me my greatest joy. I smile and laugh with them daily—it's the best medicine for a broken heart. Through it all, God sustained me then and sustains me now, reminding me that beauty can rise from ashes if I allow it.

So, as I carry forward the legacies, love, and stories of my family—anchored in the strength instilled in me, 'Armstrong strength'—I do so like a phoenix rising from the ashes, determined to use my story for good.

CHAPTER 4

A Love That Transcends Time and Space

by Ingrid M. Dalton

Ingrid M. Dalton

Ingrid is retired and lives in Georgia, USA, with her three cats. She practices and teaches Reiki and is a sensitive and medium. Ingrid loves writing, traveling, and spending time with family and friends. Contact her at: anamcara-reiki@hotmail.com

A LOVE THAT TRANSCENDS TIME AND SPACE

BY INGRID M. DALTON

In 2018, my beloved husband and soulmate, James, was diagnosed with Motor Neuron Disease, "ALS". James had recently retired, and we had planned to return to Ireland, his homeland. On the way out from the neurologist's office, the first remark that my dearest love made to me was, "I am so sorry, Precious, you were so looking forward to retirement, and now I'm sick, and we can't make that move to Ireland."

My instinctive response was, "We will be going through this journey together. Our undying love will be unshaken whatever will face us, and I will take care of you."

We had met later in life. We were together for 21 years, married for 19, and we were true soulmates. Our lives before we met were different; ending up together was divine timing. James was a catholic priest, and I was a divorcee with a family, working for the church. James and I found each other and started our amazing life together.

It is important to provide an insight into our lives to understand our journey with ALS. Since childhood, I have seen and experienced occurrences that I thought were a normal part of life. Throughout my teenage years and adulthood, I experienced premonitions and psychic abilities. Then, in my late forties, I surrendered to my spiritual awakening and embraced more metaphysical and esoteric practices.

My longing for expansion in spirituality rather than dogmatic teachings increased strongly. During our courtship, I mentioned to James about my abilities and asked him if he had an issue with it since the church's teaching does not agree with such practices. His answer was simply this: "Why would it bother me? I love you, and this is a part of who you are, and I trust you."

When we lived in Ireland, I was introduced to Reiki Healing. James came on this journey, and we both became Reiki I and Reiki II practitioners. I became a Reiki Master/Teacher. Reiki became an integral part of our lives and enhanced us spiritually. Additionally, for me, the psychic abilities and visions accelerated during Reiki sessions, and over the years, mediumship became a common custom for me.

James had a natural way of healing; he made people feel at ease and cared for. His compassion was a gift. In Ireland, he taught in high school and served as a military chaplain with the Irish peace-keeping unit in Lebanon. After we married, he continued as a hospital chaplain, extending his studies in interfaith chaplaincy across cultures. He ministered to patients in the hospital, was a grief counsellor to their families, an interfaith pastor in assisted-living facilities, a hospice chaplain, and a spiritual counselor in the psychiatric department of the hospital until his retirement.

Once diagnosed with ALS, he knew exactly what he was facing. He had witnessed how dignity and care for patients were, at times, neglected. Care at home was of utmost importance, and the hope was to transition to our home. The illness progressed rapidly.

James never once complained, never asked "Why me?"; rather, "Why not me?" Whenever his body or limbs weakened, he focused on what still worked. His legs became weaker, but he could move along with a walker. I was at his side, supporting him. In late 2018, he was fitted for a specialized wheelchair. I helped him to bed and turned him from side to side.

A physical therapist visited once per week to show James and me how to manage. Soon this ended, since as per the health insurance, there was no sign of improvement. ALS was not considered an "illness";

the cause is still not known, and home help was not covered by the health insurance until towards the end, when hospice was required. I loved caring for my husband. The doctors and nursing teams were beyond kind and informative. Without help from our friends and neighbors, it would have been impossible to carry the burden of care alone.

Our neighbors across the street became an integral part of our lives. They are practicing Muslims, and their love for their neighbor is taken seriously. For three and a half years, our neighbor came once or twice a day to assist James in bed. He helped me to move James with a hoist from the wheelchair to the bed and was always available when needed. Both men became closer as friends and true brothers. They conversed and prayed together every day. His wife would bring meals on special occasions and make us feel loved.

Another close friend helped me with the housekeeping, so I could concentrate on James. She also helped me with James. We had family and very close friends visiting from abroad. James's colleagues and former classmates visited, and our local friends helped with shopping. Then came Covid. We had to limit the people entering our home; even James's best friends had to stay away.

James could no longer tolerate the drive to his appointments in Atlanta. For blood tests, I arranged medical transport to the local doctor's office, which was exhausting for James; it took a couple of hours to get ready. With Covid came a bright light; we were able to rejoin the Atlanta medical team via Zoom and were elated to "see" our team regularly again. A close friend, a retired nurse, could bring James's vaccines and administer them. For James and me, Covid was a blessing as we talked and planned our time for important issues.

His care became physically more strenuous. I lifted James in and out of bed when we received the hoist. I maneuvered him from the bed to the wheelchair and vice versa. I turned him in bed, bathed him, massaged him, and administered his medication. I also exercised his arms and legs, since he lost all movement by then. James used a breathing machine, and by the end of 2020, he needed it all the time.

His body had weakened, but not his spirit. His various interests were still acute. I read to him. We loved to watch sports, news, educational series, and movies on TV. We had access to Irish news and sports reports, bringing his beloved homeland to our home.

During Covid our ReikiShare group and metaphysical group came to a halt. James was added to the prayer lists in churches, here and abroad, at the local mosque and the local synagogue. Reiki and every good thought helped James to "carry his cross" and me to keep the strength and to share in his suffering.

By 2021, James's health deteriorated rapidly. On March 17th, St. Patrick's Day, he was fitted with a feeding tube. The procedure needed to be performed early, or the patient would starve to death. Once diagnosed with ALS, any kind of surgery is not allowed, as it can accelerate the disease, and the chances of suffocation rise. James adjusted very well, and I was instructed how to use and clean the device. By Easter, three meals per day were administered.

Throughout our marriage, communication with each other was most important. We shared everything. I asked James if he was afraid of dying. His answer was NO. Dying is as natural as being born, but unfortunately, even those with faith have an unnatural view of it. We believed in the afterlife, Heaven, and that we would be reunited with our loved ones. James had an unshakable and profound faith in a loving God. During the night, I would hold on to James very tight, praying and hoping for the miracle of healing of his body. But his healing was of another kind. The way he accepted suffering was a miracle, and the way he left this world was another miracle.

In May, James asked for palliative care. His body was weary. The Columbus Hospice nurse arrived and was assigned until his passing. A hospital bed was used; James couldn't remain in our bed, a traumatic experience to be separated for the first time. I always slept facing James, and it took only two steps to be at his side.

James had to be turned every two hours around the clock. In those final weeks, the word sleep became foreign. The nights became short between turning, bathroom needs, and medication administration. I seldom had more than one or two hours of sleep. James couldn't be left alone. Despite the breathing machine, his lack of movement could be dangerous.

James prepared for his departure from this world. Whenever family or friends called, he thanked them personally for their part in his life and for the good memories they shared and said his farewell. His two close priest friends visited daily and every evening read poetry or chapters from a book of Irish poets and writers, closing with a prayer.

James asked me to write down everything that was needed for his passing. He prepared his obituary, one for the U.S. and one for the Irish newspaper. He arranged his entire church service, asking his priest friend to celebrate the Mass and give the homily/eulogy. Every reading, prayer, and song was carefully selected. It was both our wish to be cremated, and I keep James's urn at our home; when my time comes, our ashes will be co-mingled. James asked me if I would say a few words at his funeral service, and I responded that I didn't think I could do it. Confidently, James assured me that I could do it – and I did.

We knew many people couldn't attend his funeral due to Covid. James's family couldn't travel to the U.S., yet he correctly figured out how many people would be able to participate and join the meal afterwards.

So far, the only medication James took for pain was Tylenol, but as the pain increased, he was introduced to morphine. Before sponge bathing, washing hair, or before the insertion of a catheter, an anti-anxiety medication was added. I took care of the hourly medication intake.

The miracle I mentioned earlier was granted to James, how he could leave this world. The cause of death for ALS patients is suffocation; the greatest fear for the patient, caregiver, and family. Not only does morphine diminish pain, but it also keeps the airways open. Suddenly, in the last eight days, James was breathing on his own, using the breathing machine less. The painful mask could be removed.

Shortly before his transition, James asked me to hold his hands and told me that the easiest decision he had made in his life was marrying me. I sensed that in his final weeks, he was reviewing his life, sharing his thoughts with me. He was at peace and concluding his life. In the final four days, he was mostly sleeping, and in the last two days, unconscious. I was taught how to recognize signs of pain when a person is unconscious and decide on increased pain medication.

On August 9th, 2021, at 5:00 a.m., as I gave James the morphine, I knew it was the day he would leave us. I had "seen" his parents for weeks, coming closer to greet their beloved son on the other side. James saw them too. I gave him a gentle wash and prepared him for his journey. I sat by him, my head next to his, holding him in my arms, telling him that it was okay to let go and that Jesus, his parents, and loved ones were waiting for him; thanking him for the happiest years and for our love. The device clipped to his index finger displayed his pulse and oxygen level. As I held him, I observed it slowing down. At 8:30 a.m., the heart stopped, and the love of my life transitioned peacefully into his eternal home, free from all suffering, his gentle soul soaring.

The coming days and weeks were surreal. The well-planned funeral and paperwork kept me occupied, but grief was insurmountable. This mixture of emotions had to be experienced, the five steps described by grief counselors as Denial, Anger, Bargaining, Depression, and Acceptance. There is also Anticipating Grief, but I did not endure as such. James had prepared me well. I had enormous support; my family and dear friends helped me in this long journey to a breakthrough. The anticipated grief, the mourning that occurs before an expected loss, is common with terminal illness, and it protected me from the steps of grief.

With depression, I had no feeling of hopelessness but profound sadness. Grief is personal and an individual experience. It never goes away; one learns to adjust to a different reality. I grieved profoundly and still grieve.

In his final year, James told me that he wanted me to have a happy life after he's gone. My response was, "How can I ever be happy without you?" And he said, "It's just a different kind of happy." At that time, it was not negotiable for me. So, what was and still is the breakthrough? It is the result of allowing grief to take its natural course, the physical and emotional pain. When all of a sudden it hits me how much

I miss him, and I have to catch my breath, I am so sad and cry so profoundly that I think I am having a heart attack. In the beginning, this occurred often, and sometimes I needed to call a close friend to help me through. Over the years, it has become less, yet it is still acute at times.

Writing and traveling have helped me significantly. After James's passing, I travelled to Ireland to thank family and friends for their support during his illness. It was also a healing journey, as we shared stories. Being back home where we lived brought reassuring, happy memories. Since then, I've travelled frequently, visiting with family and friends and going to new places. James and I were enthusiastic travelers, and I find solace in it.

I also became certified as a death doula, assisting people as they cross over. I joined Elias's group and attended a retreat. This brings me to the metaphysical and spiritual part of my transformation. Since James's transition, I can communicate with him, not only knowing that he is around, but hearing him, feeling him, and at times his scent. James is around me all the time. He is protecting me via the other side, advising me, and he's traveling with me for free. This gives me the confidence and courage to keep on living that happy life that my soulmate referred to.

My future looks bright again because I'm dedicating my time to matters that are close to my heart: my Reiki practice, facilitating our local metaphysical group, writing, traveling, spending time with family and dear friends that James and I shared. Whatever time I have left on this plane, I will use wisely and, as James and I shared, to promote love and peace to this world.

In closing, I am convinced that when my time to transition comes, my dearest James will be awaiting me in a sublime new existence where together our souls and spirits can soar.

CHAPTER 5

From Fear to Faith

by Hugh Imhof

Hugh Imhof

Hugh Imhoff is a certified coach, helping men and women through life's challenges and transformation. Hugh has thirty-five years of sobriety, has been cigarette-free for thirteen years, overcame cancer in 2012 and was a long-distance cyclist from 2014 through 2017. He has six century rides to his credit. Hugh is working on his first book, *Sobriety and Beyond: Creating a Life of Purpose and Happiness.*

If you like this story, Hugh hopes that you will check out his story, *I Chose to Live,* found in the collaboration, *The Resilient Heart.* Please share these stories with anyone you feel may benefit. Thank you.

Email at Newhugh59@gmail.com

FROM FEAR TO FAITH

BY HUGH IMHOF

On judgment day, God will judge you, and those who are unworthy will suffer eternal damnation!

Our priest at Catholic mass was always warning us about what happens to sinners. Fearing God was mandatory.

Was being forced to go to church or living in fear a requirement to receive God's love? It seemed like it. It didn't take long before my younger brothers and I grabbed the pamphlet from the Sunday service and walked to the drug store instead of staying for mass. I would watch people's actions during the week. They seemed like hypocrites to me. Going to church on Sunday in their best clothes and then during the week they would be mean to others and do seemingly whatever they wanted. Our priest always ended the sermon with, go forth and sin no more. Churchgoers' actions said, go forth and sin some more. At age sixteen, I told my mom I no longer wanted to go to church. She reluctantly agreed.

I was running away from a very early age. I started smoking as a teenager. It was my I'll show you attitude towards authority. Nuns and brothers in school were the worst. It seemed their sole purpose was to discover something wrong with you or something about your behavior that needed correcting. I remember being slapped across the face when I didn't respond to my name being called during homeroom. I also recall being asked to explain what the holy trinity was in front of a high school class. When I was finished, the nun spent ten minutes ridiculing me in front of everyone. She completed her tirade by asking, you call yourself a Christian. I replied with, no, I am forced to be Catholic. You could have heard a pin drop after that. She just glared at me.

I also would drink alcohol at every opportunity. Even if I had to steal it from my parents. When I was permitted to drink beer at events like wedding receptions, I'd always drink more than I was supposed to. My tolerance for alcohol was very high early on. In college, I drank a couple of nights a week. I usually drink until I get drunk. When I joined the Navy, my drinking only increased. I went out for several nights almost every week. When I left the Navy, I drank every day for seven years. I would drink until I was drunk or passed out.

No matter where I was or who I was with, there was always someone trying to get me to slow down with the drinking or moderate. I got hit by a car at the Great Lakes Naval Base. I had a broken left pinky finger, but I didn't feel it until the doctor at the Base Hospital put it back in place. He told me that he couldn't believe that I was even alive, given my blood-alcohol level. I paid no heed to that warning. The last four days of my drinking were spent in a blackout. I could only remember bits and pieces of what I did, where I went, and who I was with. I had a problem. I needed help. I went to Alcoholics Anonymous.

I read a book called Came to Believe. This book had stories of other alcoholics finding faith in a higher power. It caused me to start contemplating God or the universal spirit. Who kept sending me messengers telling me I needed help? Who kept me from alcoholic poisoning or a wet brain? Who was watching over me, helping me get back home after a night of drinking? Someone or something was looking out for me.

When I first got sober, I wasn't drinking, but I was hanging on to sobriety by my fingernails. I got down on my knees and asked God to remove the obsession to drink from me. I don't know exactly when it happened, but I did start feeling different, better. The desire to drink had lessened considerably.

I started going to a Christian church. I went to mass every Sunday. I joined a bible study group and entered a discipleship with another

Christian. I even got re-baptized as an adult. After one year, I was getting very frustrated. It seemed like a lot of people at that church were judging me and not accepting me. It was as if I was one of them, but perhaps I was too much of a sinner for them. It was very strange and very hurtful. So, I walked away from that church never to return.

God is God-made, and religion is man-made. This thought flashed through my brain like a lightning strike. I could talk to God whenever, wherever I wanted. I read many books about different philosophies and beliefs. I started formulating my own spirituality. I spent hours walking in the woods and forest preserves. I experienced nature at every possible level. I know I was viewing some of the universal spirit's handiwork. Utterly amazing. I thought about all the times that the results of things I did and experienced could have ended much worse than they did. I contemplated the lessons that I'd learned and the opportunities to adjust how I thought, felt, and acted. The concepts of just being, accepting people and things as they were without judgement and staying in the present became pillars in my life. I, and everyone else, are exactly where we are supposed to be. We are perfect in our own imperfection. There was a reason for all that had happened. To trust in the unknown and the unseen seemed to be relevant. Could the millions of people of faith be misled or wrong? I could not believe that. Souls that left their human bodies were everywhere, guiding and helping me and others. I no longer believe in coincidence.

I recalled walking down the street one day. I was approaching an alley tucked between two large buildings. I suddenly stopped for no apparent reason. A car came flying out of the alley at a ridiculous speed. I didn't hear anything. I could have been seriously injured or killed. Grace.

Eventually, I quit smoking. Once again, I asked God for his help. I asked him to remove the obsession with smoking from me. He answered. I haven't had a drink since I quit back in 1989, and haven't had a cigarette since I quit in 2012.

I worked for the Electrical Union for several years. I absolutely loved the work. Unfortunately, I was laid off a few times. Each time I was laid off was for a longer duration. Finally, I left the union. One day I received a call from a company at O'Hare airport. I interviewed with them and was hired. They said I needed to take a pre-employment physical. So, I went to a doctor to get that done. He said that they found blood in my urine, and further testing was recommended. Several tests were performed. A CT scan revealed a cancerous mass attached to my left kidney. The cancer has destroyed my left kidney. The doctor said it was serendipitous that they even found the cancer. Surgery was scheduled. I believed that the cancer was a warning. I believed that there was a reason why I got the news early on, before the cancer metastasized. The surgery was successful. They removed the cancer and the remnants of my kidney. I had to return for annual scans, but the cancer never came back. It was another miracle in my life. Keep in mind that if I stayed with the Electrical Union and worked for another union contractor, I would not have been asked to get the physical. I would have died in 2015.

I did a lot of dating over many years, but it seemed like I could never find the right person. I took inventories of my behavior at the end of each relationship. I continued to learn and grow as a person and prospective partner. I went on a six-year hiatus from dating. I spent a lot of time by myself, with God and in nature. I started talking to God about wanting to find a companion. I was very specific about what values she ought to have, what we would enjoy doing together. I visualized us supporting each other and being loyal to each other. I saw us being on the same emotional maturity level. I visualized us doing many things, enjoying each other's company, and I expressed gratitude as if we were already together and experiencing life together. Within a short time, I got an email from a dating website. Someone liked me and sent me a message. I read the message, looked at her pictures and read her profile. I responded to the message. We messaged back and forth a few times and then she sent me her phone number. Our first phone call was three hours long. Our first date was like a homecoming. Our values were identical. We could have serious conversations, and we could laugh and have fun. Honesty, openness and vulnerability simply flowed. I told her that I wanted to continue seeing her, but that I had been hurt very badly by a group of people in the past and didn't want to be hurt again. She asked me to trust her. I did. Our relationship was about love and faith. We have been together now for nearly seven years. We have been married for nearly three years. It is the best relationship I've ever had. Lynne is the most wonderful woman I've ever known. She loves me at a level I've never experienced from any other human being. We have faith in each other and that we will stay the same essential person we are today. Our love is only transcended by the love of God.

The faith I have today has been built on a lifetime of trial and error. Every time I have sought God out, he has answered. Yes, I took a lot of action. Yet I believe faith without works is dead. I am doing a lot of writing these days. I'm working on my first book; this is my fourth chapter that will be entered into a collaborative effort. I have some ideas for two other books. I am hoping to send God's love to others by helping them through my writing and coaching.

I hope that you will find faith and grow in faith as I have. I could not live, nor would I have survived without it. I hope that the faith that develops within you will help you live your best life as the best version of yourself. God can be anything or anyone you want him or it to be. God, universal spirit, God as I understand him, Muhammad, Allah or universal intelligence all work for me. The choice is yours. May strong faith be yours.

CHAPTER 6

Keeper of the Stars

by Joy Klavenga

Joy Klavenga

Joy Klavenga has lived the kind of life that doesn't allow for pretending. She has survived trauma, hardship, loss, and the kind of breaking points that strip a person down to their bones. Her strength wasn't inherited or taught—it was carved out of necessity, one hard lesson at a time.

She has spent years standing beside people fighting their own battles, offering the same fierce compassion she once had to learn to give herself. She understands survival from both sides—the aching hunger at the bottom and the dizzying air at the top—she knows both shape a person.

Now, as the full-time caregiver to her husband, Joy continues to love with a depth forged in fire. Her writing is unfiltered, real, and anchored in lived truth. She has lived the lows and the highs—and she considers both a blessing.

KEEPER OF THE STARS

BY JOY KLAVENGA

I didn't know the moment my life split into before and after. Most people imagine a breakdown as something loud or obvious, something you witness in slow motion. Mine arrived quietly, disguised as ordinary days.

It was the small shifts that first whispered the truth: the way Tim repeated the same question minutes apart, the way he stared a little too long at nothing, the way the warmth behind his eyes flickered, then dimmed, then returned, then dimmed again. At first, I blamed myself. I told myself I was tired, unkind, imagining things. I convinced myself that maybe it was me who had changed, that maybe I was the one withdrawing, losing patience, losing softness, losing something essential.

That is one of the cruelest parts of loving someone through change: you begin by doubting yourself. You explain away what you see because the truth feels too big, too painful, too impossible to name. I made excuses. I told myself he was distracted. Stress. Age. A rough week. Anything but what my spirit already knew. Deep down, a quiet knowing was rising in me, and I kept pushing it back down because I was not ready for what it was asking me to face.

But then came the moment I saw it, the emptiness behind his eyes that didn't belong to him. Tim had always been simple in his own way, direct, literal, sometimes tuned out, but never hollow. Never gone. When I looked at him that day, really looked, I felt a jolt of fear so sharp that I had to steady myself on the counter. Something was wrong. Something serious. And for the first time in our marriage, I realized that I would have to be the one to say it out loud.

I had been the messenger of painful truths his whole life, news of deaths, disappointments, betrayals, changes. I was always the one people told first, and therefore always the one who had to carry the news to him. But this time, the words I had to speak were heavier, sharper, crueler than anything I had ever had to say. I didn't know how to tell him that his mind was slipping away. That something inside him wasn't connecting anymore. That the man who once walked into Casey's gas station and made my heart fall straight into my stomach was beginning to fade.

I still remember that version of him so clearly. The way he moved. The way he smiled. The way something in me recognized something in him before I could explain it. Love does not always arrive with fireworks. Sometimes it arrives as a knowing, as a pull, as a sudden awareness that your life is about to be changed by another person's presence. That was Tim for me. He was familiar before he was even mine. Maybe that is why watching him disappear has felt like losing a part of my own language.

One afternoon, he looked at me with a softness I hadn't seen in years, and I realized the truth: my love for him was still alive, fierce, loyal, unfiltered. It had simply been buried under exhaustion, resentment, survival, and the thousand tiny cuts of daily life.

Caregiving has a way of covering love in layers of fatigue. Not because the love is gone, but because survival gets louder. You stop reaching for tenderness when you are just trying to get through the day. You stop feeling your own heart because you are too busy holding everything together.

When he began talking about people trying to kill us and insisted that we were in danger across the street, the ground shifted under my feet. I drove him to the hospital. They kept him for three weeks.

While he was gone, I rested for the first time in years. My body shut down on me; I slept as if the world had finally set down a weight I'd been carrying too long. I watched what I wanted, ate when I wanted, and did nothing when I wanted. The house was quiet in a way I had forgotten was possible. No tension in the air. No constant scanning. No listening for what might happen next. And I hated that it felt good. That is a kind of guilt no one prepares you for, the relief that comes with losing what you love.

The rest felt honest, but it also felt wrong. I did not miss the chaos, but I missed the man. I missed the version of us that still felt reachable. I missed what had been, even while my body was grateful for the pause. Two truths can live in the same heart at once: I was tired beyond words, and I loved him beyond reason.

But when I visited him, I saw a man who had withered. A man who was becoming unrecognizable. And all at once, every bit of rest, every moment of quiet, felt like a betrayal. Others told me it wasn't my responsibility, that I had choices, that I didn't have to stay. They said it like freedom. They said it like permission. For someone else, it would have been. But I knew they were wrong for me. Tim had lived his whole life with people leaving him. I would not be another person who walked away.

Not because I was trapped. Not because I had no options. But because love, for me, had never been about convenience. It had never been about staying only while things were easy, clear, mutual, or rewarding. Love is a vow we make with our lives, not just our words. And mine was this: I will not abandon you inside your unraveling.

One night, weeks later, I found myself standing in the kitchen listening to a man on TikTok singing "Keeper of the Stars." My eyes filled with tears before I could stop them. The grief of loving someone who is slipping away is a grief that lives in the bones.

It is not always loud. Sometimes it sits quietly in the body until a song, a smell, a look, or a memory reaches in and pulls it to the surface.

I didn't hear Tim come in. He placed his hand gently on my arm and, without a word, pulled me into a slow dance right there in the kitchen. His face softened. His smile was the same smile I fell in love with. For those few minutes, time rewound. For those few minutes, I had my husband back.

When the song ended, I pulled back to look at him, and for a heartbeat, the world was perfect. Then his expression changed, clouded, confused, distant. He looked past me, not at me. And as if the universe itself wanted to puncture the moment, the memory of another song rose in my mind: "The Dance." The price of loving him was always going to be this right here, knowing that I would cherish moments that were already turning into memories while he was forgetting them.

But even then, I realized something: I would choose this life again. I would choose him again. I would choose the joy, the heartbreak, the confusion, the dance, the slow unraveling, the long goodbye. Because love is not the absence of pain, love is the courage to walk into pain with your heart still open.

Now I stand in a place I never imagined. I know Tim will forget me. I know I will lose him in pieces, not all at once, first his memories, then his stories, then his expressions, then his recognition, and finally his presence in the world I still must live in. He will vanish like fog burning off at sunrise. But I will remain. And I will carry him. Because even if one day he no longer knows my name, I will still remember the man who loved me before he lost the ability to love anything at all.

This has changed me, too. It has taught me that a breakthrough does not always come as healing or rescue. Sometimes it comes in becoming someone who can stand in heartbreak, stay open, and still choose love.

I will be the keeper of our stars. I will be the witness to our dance. And when the final moment arrives, when the last light leaves his eyes, I will love him still.

Because that is what love is.

Not romance.
But the witness.
The keeper of what once burned bright.

The one who stays when the music fades and carries the stars home alone.

CHAPTER 7

From The Ashes

by Sarah Elizabeth

Sarah Elizabeth

Sarah Elizabeth is an evidential psychic medium, intuitive healing facilitator, and grief coach dedicated to supporting others through loss, healing, and personal transformation. Drawing from lived experience and a lifelong awareness of the spirit world, she creates compassionate, grounded spaces where people can reconnect with their intuition and the love that continues beyond loss. Internationally trusted for her work, Sarah blends intuitive insight with emotional support, empowering individuals to move forward with clarity, resilience, and confidence in their own inner guidance.

FROM THE ASHES: CULTIVATING COMMUNITY FROM DESTRUCTION

BY SARAH ELIZABETH

At 24 years old, I found myself standing in the dimly lit shower of a sterile, unfamiliar hotel room, which was now my new home, repeating a mantra shakily under my breath as the water gently ran over my face. "Do not let this destroy you." It was a statement, better yet, a prayer, that was never intended to be under my ownership. I repeated it to myself on a constant loop, in hopes that somewhere in my psyche, it would solidify. It was followed by a stark reminder to myself: "There was a fire. Brendan is dead." This statement, paired with the first, was repeated as many times as I felt necessary to convince myself that yes, a nightmare had become reality. As I stood in the shower and ran my head under its water, I subconsciously asked far too much of it. I pleaded for it to cleanse away something that rarely washes out with anything. Death.

My mantra, as mentioned, was never meant for me at all. Initially, it was what I whispered into the ear of and asked of my partner, Brendan, as he lay in the ICU in a medically induced coma. Our apartment caught fire, and he had fallen three stories out of the window as flames ravaged around him. Although the aforementioned phrase may appear to be a statement, it was an ask, a plea. Please, fight. Live. Come back from this. Come back to me. Please, do not give up. Please, overcome this. Unsure if he could hear me in his comatose state, I asked this of him anyway, every single day.

Brendan would wake up from his coma and persevere through multiple rounds of surgery and many other medical hurdles, but would pass away on April 3rd, 2022. His death was the turning point in my own personal journey. It was at this moment that what I had asked of him, I would now need to ask of myself. The first few days of my loss are comprised solely of blurry, grief-clouded memories. I recall being stuck in a cycle of scream-crying in bed, subsequently passing out, and waking up screaming again in a horrific, torturous loop. I cannot tell you exactly how long this cycle went on, only my first memory of me standing in that shower after it subsided. "Do not let this destroy you."

Achieving the goal of this statement felt like asking the impossible of myself. I had lost everything. My home and personal belongings were destroyed, my partner was no longer on this earth, and most of his possessions (things one would typically have in remembrance of their deceased loved one) were gone with the fire as well. The weight of the losses was immeasurable. The pain felt like a hot knife in my chest, something I instantly learned was a *literal, real* occurrence, and not merely a figure of speech used to measure the pain of grief. When the simple act of breathing feels like an uphill battle, how is one supposed to then live and move forward?

Looking back on it, my initial chosen method of moving through my grief seemed second nature. It didn't feel like a choice at all, but rather an innate knowledge of something I must do. 10 days after Brendan's passing, I posted my first video to TikTok, a platform I had only ever been a silent viewer on before. The video was shaky and admittedly a bit awkward, but it was an act I had a deep reverence for pursuing. I set my phone on top of the AC unit in my hotel room-turned home, clicked record, and said the following to anyone who would listen: "I am about to describe a situation that I never, ever thought I would have to live through. On April 3rd, I unexpectedly lost my partner. And on March 8th, about a month before, we experienced a devastating apartment fire and lost everything. When the fire happened, I thought that was the worst it could get, that this was a big moment in life that was going to change me forever. And then, my partner died. I am realizing that it's helping me to look online, to find other people's stories, to hear from those who are also going through something extremely hard. I don't have a lot to give in terms of advice or teachings, but I do have empathy, and I do have space. For some reason, I have this really big urge to speak online about what I'm going through, in hopes that I can help other people. My loss will be different from your loss, but some of that pain that we feel is shared. If I can be someone who helps you–or maybe we can help each other–then I'm grateful for that. I'm 24 years old, and I have experienced two of the worst things that some people will go through: the loss of a significant other and a devastating house fire. As far as I know, that's not normal. So, I want to be a part of a conversation about things that aren't normal that happen to people."

That initial social media video was my first endeavor into not letting my grief destroy me. It was my own personal, public protest, one that demanded, Something good *will* come out of this. And that, it did. I continued to post daily, utilizing my social media page as a public journal. My page was a call to others suffering through loss, inviting anyone to join me in the tumultuous journey that is healing. Additionally, the thought was that if I got myself up out of bed to make a video about my grief each day, then that was one more day of me moving through the blanket of devastation I was facing. From then on, every video I posted brought a new one-on-one interaction, a new stranger who shared their own story with me, and a new building block to a growing community. These interactions became another life raft in the sea of grief that dared to swallow me whole. There was a definitive moment in my journey when I looked around and realized that I wasn't alone. A realization that if strangers could root for me, I could root for myself, too. I kept posting, and today, what started as an online journal for me has now turned into a real-world career, where I spend my days helping others feel seen and heard in their own grief journey through a professional approach. For that, I am beyond grateful.

What I learned through this process is that community is the key to surviving hardship. Before my loss, I was the kind of person who toughed it out on her own. I could do hard things, I could take care of myself. I was, and occasionally still am, the type to want to shut out the world and endure the low moments by myself. However, grief wastes no time in reminding you that it does not reward loneliness and isolation.

Although I am proud of myself for the action I took to keep showing up for myself in my grief, it is truly the shared community I must thank. It transformed me in ways I will never be able to properly describe or show gratitude for. To be clear, my gratitude for the community applies to both the offline and the online world. Though I found a remarkable kind of community in social media, I must make it clear that it is not the format that is to be highlighted; it's the act of simply showing up and being present for each other. In the end, my grief *did* destroy me. It broke me down, stripped me bare, and unveiled emotional states I could hardly even conceptualize. While this may be true, I did not *remain* destroyed by grief. Through the pairing of two distinct actions, showing up for myself and my community showing up for me, I survived. Both close loved ones and strangers alike showed genuine support in ways I could have never expected. After my loss, I was unsteady, akin to a broken, wobbly chair that never sat right, one that wobbled back and forth due to a leg that was too loose or too short on one side. As for my community, their showing up for me was the small pieces of paper folded underneath a too-short leg, a simple gesture with a great impact on stability. My experiences in grief and loss taught me that sometimes, to be dismantled and seemingly destroyed by life is not the end-all be-all. The transformation and love that follow the destruction may astound you in the rarest of ways, and that is something to look forward to.

CHAPTER 8

The Day the Door Closed and the Universe Opened

by Natalie LaChance

Natalie LaChance

Natalie LaChance, the heart and visionary behind **Nati Love's Creations**, is a multifaceted creative entrepreneur, storyteller, and soul-led maker whose work blends art, intuition, and purpose. After navigating a major life transition following a 26-year corporate career, Natalie answered a deeper calling: to create, heal, and inspire through authenticity and love.

Through Nati Love's Creations, she brings ideas to life using epoxy resin, jewelry design, affirmations, EFT tapping, and intentional storytelling. Each creation is infused with meaning, emotional connection, and the belief that beauty can be both seen and felt. Natalie's work is rooted in resilience, self-discovery, and the courage to rebuild from uncertainty while honoring intuition and inner wisdom.

A devoted wife, mother, and homeschool advocate, Natalie weaves her lived experiences into everything she creates, offering encouragement to others navigating change, loss, reinvention, and growth. Her voice is warm, honest, and empowering, reminding others that transformation is not only possible but purposeful.

Natalie's chapter in this book reflects her journey from breakdown to breakthrough, inviting readers to trust their path, reclaim their creative power, and remember that even in the midst of uncertainty, love, light, and possibility are always being created.

THE DAY THE DOOR CLOSED AND THE UNIVERSE OPENED

BY NATALIE LACHANCE

The morning I was laid off didn't feel like an explosion; it felt like a quiet click. One moment, I sat in my home office, surrounded by the familiar hum of my computer and a half-empty mug of coffee I'd reheated twice. Next, I was staring at a calendar invite from someone I barely knew, not my manager, not my director, but a name that had become all too familiar during our company's annual realignment.

After twenty-six years in corporate America, I knew exactly what that meant.

I joined the video call, the polite corporate tone filling the space where my heartbeat should have been. The words were rehearsed: "restructuring"; "transition"; "we appreciate your years of service." I had heard the same phrases whispered in the virtual hallways the year before, and the year before that. But this time, they were meant for me.

Oddly, I wasn't angry. I wasn't even surprised. What I felt was stillness.

It was as if time had stopped, and in that frozen silence I heard something deeper, a soft inner voice that said, *You knew this door was closing. It's time to open the one meant for you.*

I logged off, sat back in my chair, and took a long breath. There were no tears. Just peace, the kind that comes when your spirit recognizes what your mind hasn't caught up to yet.

For the first time in decades, I didn't have a meeting to attend, a report to finish, or a project to manage. I had no title, no deadlines, and no roadmap. Just me.

And that's when the fear crept in.

What now? How would I contribute? Who was I without this identity I had worn for half my life?

I wandered through those first days like a ghost in my own home. My daughter's laughter from the other room was both comforting and foreign. My husband's attempts to cheer me up only reminded me of how uncertain everything suddenly felt. I was free, yes, but freedom can feel terrifying when you've lived by structure for so long.

Then one morning, sitting on the back deck watching the sunrise, something shifted.

The light spilled through the trees in gold streaks, warm and alive, and it touched everything, even the parts of me that felt broken. I remember whispering, "If this is my blank page, then I'm going to fill it with color."

That single thought became my turning point.

I began to reconnect with the parts of me I had buried beneath years of corporate expectations, the creative, curious, spiritual woman who once believed she could shape energy with her hands and her heart. I picked up resin, paints, crystals, and affirmations. I began crafting not for profit or productivity, but for peace.

And in those early creations, I found something sacred: *joy.*

At first, my projects were small—coasters, candles, little charms filled with color and intention. But every piece carried a vibration. I would say affirmations as I poured: *I am safe. I am guided. I am creating beauty from what once felt broken.*

Each finished piece wasn't just art; it was a reminder that I was healing.

That's how Nati Love's Creations was born, not from a business plan but from a soul calling.

The more I created, the more I shared, and the more people began to connect. What started as a quiet act of healing became a movement of energy through TikTok lives, through community, through laughter, and shared stories of transformation.

I realized that the breakdown wasn't punishment. It was preparation.

Because when everything I had built around me fell away, I discovered that my real foundation was never the job, the paycheck, or the title. It was a *purpose.*

That purpose now shows up in everything I do, from crafting art infused with affirmations to guiding others through EFT tapping and Hoʻoponopono, to speaking words of hope to people navigating their own storms. I've learned that transformation doesn't always roar in like thunder; sometimes it arrives as a whisper that says, "You are more than this moment. Trust the unfolding."

Looking back, I can see that the layoff wasn't the end of my story. It was the universe gently redirecting me toward alignment, showing me that when one door closes, it's not rejection; it's redirection.

The hardest part of transformation is surrender, releasing control long enough for grace to enter.

In that surrender, I found myself again.

Now, every time I sit at my crafting table, I feel the echo of that day, the click of the door closing, and the light that rushed in afterward. The universe didn't take my security away; it gave me a new sense of power.

I no longer measure my worth by titles or timelines. I measure it by peace, purpose, and the ripple of light my creations leave in the world.

So when people ask if I'd go back—if I'd undo that moment in my home office when a stranger delivered news that changed my life—I smile and say, "No. That was the day the universe handed me back to myself."

Because sometimes, the most beautiful beginnings are disguised as endings.

And sometimes, the door that closes behind you is the very one that lets the light in.

CHAPTER 9

I Let the Dam Break

by Amy Lay

Amy Lay

Amy Lay, known as The INVINCIBILITY Coach, is a mental and performance specialist who is deeply embedded in the non-physical magic that floods and forms our physical existence. Amy is a catalyst and lives authentically in her critical talent and creativity for social alchemy. Her clients exist in all disciplines, industries, and sectors, and are high-achieving and ambitious doers and makers of great things. She unlocks self-confidence and introduces dimensions well beyond conscious understanding through emotional control, self-regulation, and the establishment of a new baseline of peace. Amy is the calm and quiet *eye of the storm,* and she's ready to help you get there, too.

https://theinvincibilitycoach.com/
https://www.linkedin.com/in/amy-lay-91a87610/
https://www.instagram.com/theinvincibilitycoach/

https://www.facebook.com/profile.php?id=61583238645706
https://www.youtube.com/@TheINVINCIBILITYCoach
https://www.amazon.com/dp/B0FJFCZLKF

I LET THE DAM BREAK

BY AMY LAY

I remember the ambulance lights flashing bright blue and red through the row of windows in front of my grandmother's house in rural South Dakota; through the screened-in porch with a carpet sample patchwork rug, through the big front tree my brother fell from years later, and the neighbor's St. Bernard bounding out their door to his rescue. I remember the lights, and I remember the oddly discomfiting peach color of the hospital walls.

When was I told? How was I told? What did I say? Did I understand?

I suppose, as happens, time passed because my next memory is the row of pews in the chapel for my father's funeral. The walls were a sort of butter yellow. It was a brain aneurysm.

How did we get his body from South Dakota to Texas? Was he already in a casket, or was it just a regular box used for air transport? Did someone in my family accompany him? Too many people in my family passed away before I was old enough to ask these questions.

My older cousin, sitting next to me at the funeral service, leaned over and said, "You know, it's okay to cry."

I remember that, but I don't remember myself. I was somehow already as stoic as a seasoned wound. I was seven years old, broken in two.

It was as if an insurmountably tall dam appeared in front of me with no way to see over or around it, and I had no will to try. I was at once in the spotlight of community pity yet lost in a sea of sorrow; I had no sense to navigate.

The cascade of days, weeks, and decades of dam building following the bursting forth of so much sorrow didn't include lessons on how to float atop the rapids of a rotting self. The joy and carefree moments so synonymous with childhood were few, and the already complex cloud of formative years became the heavy fog that filled my heart. The dam was the most reliable shield against any unknown.

I laughed, I loved, but I continued to lose so many matches with death: Family, friends, pets, and a child. I had become a professional witness to the loss of life. And a loner.

After a period of years, I began reflecting on this character that lived inside my soul. I slowly pieced together fragments of memory that would surface in the slowly rising pool at my feet, the collected drips that found their way through the cracks of my dam wall. I realized I had a clear vision of my childhood self, knowing deep in my bones that I was placed on this planet to help people. I *knew* it with every shred of my being.

Over a lifetime, I had watched the muddy water rise around me as the cracks in my dam increased in size and number. I didn't have enough fingers to block them all. I watched the other inhabitants of the pool become more and more soaked in foul moods, forlorn and furious with this thing we call life. I came to understand the darkness so many viewed as unconquerable because I knew how heavy the banner of misery could be. So I knew why they fought so desperately to poke fingers into the cracks of their own section of the dam, terrified of the ghastly unknown pressing against the other side.

Come the day, I have no memory of date or time, but I let the dam break.

I watched the walls tumble down around me. I choked and choked on fear, and then I felt lighter than air. I was floating, and I was free.

The healing seemed immediate, although I knew it was not. I was simply different.

Is this why they began coming to me? Is it because I now embodied the strength I had ascribed to the dam I allowed to burst?

I had become a rehabilitator of life, someone who others sought out for reframing, for redesign, or for carefully engineered demolition.

I came to know with all my heart that I was placed so far down, and early, in this earthly experience to understand the subtle art of lifting myself up in front of others, instead of feeling responsible for lifting *them* up. This distinction, in and of itself, took the better part of a decade or more.

It began happening everywhere I went, many times well underway before I realized it. I was helping others understand the cracks in their life that were trying to teach them about growth and expansion, encouraging them to catalyze their pain like I learned to do, not only seeing through the shadow but recruiting the inner strength necessary to walk through it instead of learning the awful skill of circumnavigating excruciating agony.

I gained confidence. I lost my fear. I gained knowledge. I lost my innocence. I gained clairsentience and claircognizance. I lost friends who were not ready to extract their fingers.

This was the advent of a soul quest to which I do not remember committing, where I agreed to embody the quiet and uncanny properties of quicksilver, alchemizing the darkness of human strife into the light of cosmic joy.

I see a world now that is crowded, shoulder to shoulder on the dry and joyless side of the dam, feeling somehow safe and sound but hopelessly parched in separation from the healing waters on the other side.

I see a world of intertwining fingers poked deep inside the cracks and holes of a wall of fear, the fracturing tower trying desperately to convince the devotees of the dam that if they would only let go and trust, the fear would be washed away.

I see a world now that dances and darts around triggers whose impact would be minimized by trusting the healing waters of the other side of the dam.

My job? I know now my job is to allow them to see that the dam is within. To see that the healing waters are also within. It is a job of observation and patience, and witness.

Within the origin of my own shadow and death, within my confusion around compassion and courage, within all my lifetime beginnings, which started with endings, I somehow emerged with an ever-clear obsession for life.

I know now, but did not know then; a breakdown must precede a breakthrough.

I know now, but did not know then; this is the same dam that rises for all souls who lose.

I know now, but did not know then, that the other side of the dam holds purification.

I am the dam, destined to be pulled apart and purified because all paths lead to my freedom.

My mission is to teach, to guide willing souls through the metamorphosis that begins with pulling fingers, one by one, out of the over-cocooning process taking place on the fear side of the dam. I speak a language of light that helps others interpret the singular map within that guarantees the transmutation of confusion and limitation to clarity and flight.

I am you.

You are me.

Let the dam burst within.

And we will be free.

CHAPTER 10

When Grief Awakened The Soul

by Kathleen Loso

Kathleen Loso

Kathleen Loso is a certified psychic medium and intuitive guide devoted to helping others find clarity, healing, and peace during life's most challenging moments. After experiencing profound personal loss and spiritual awakening, Kathleen transformed her own breakdown into a powerful breakthrough, discovering her soul's calling to serve as a bridge between the physical and spiritual worlds. Through her intuitive work, she offers compassionate insight, gentle guidance, and heartfelt messages of hope. Kathleen provides private readings and spiritual support to clients worldwide. Learn more at **kathleenloso.com** and follow her journey on social media as *Kathleen Loso Psychic Medium*.

WHEN GRIEF AWAKENED THE SOUL

BY KATHLEEN LOSO

The day I wasn't prepared for. A cold day in January at 1:31 PM. My world—my entire world—was completely shattered. I lost my dad. Suddenly. Without warning. He was always there for me, in the good times and the bad. He took care of me after my accident. I couldn't have asked for a better dad. He was my everything. And just like that, he was gone.

My life, as I knew it, was suddenly gone too. Everything felt different. I felt like I couldn't breathe. I wanted nothing more than to talk to him, even for a minute. To ask him what to do. To hear his voice. To have one more conversation. But that wasn't going to happen.

I was in disbelief. I couldn't process it. I moved around in a daze, not really present, just trying to make it through the hours. Everything felt unreal. One minute I had a dad, and the next minute I didn't. Nothing made sense.

Just going through the motions as the days passed. I wasn't fully present, and I wasn't fully myself. I felt like I was floating through the hours, doing what needed to be done, but not really processing anything. My mind was foggy, and my heart was numb. Helping my mom became my focus. She had just lost the man she shared her life with. Seeing her like that broke my heart. I wanted to be strong for her, even though inside I felt like I was falling apart.

Trying to get our lives in some type of order felt impossible. Nothing made sense. We were all hurting, and everything around us felt different now. We didn't know where to start.

Mom needed her family. Thank God I have two sisters and two brothers. We leaned on each other, cried together, and tried to get through each day.

But I needed more. Something deeper called me, something beyond the physical. I dove deep into studying, into spiritual work. It became a lifeline, a way to steady myself when the pain felt overwhelming.

As a teen, I saw many psychic mediums. They all told me I was gifted and that everything I needed was inside me. Back then, I didn't know what to do with it. Life happened, and I never fully stepped into it.

Now it was my time. Losing my dad changed everything. I had to trust the gift that had always been there. I knew it was time to step into who I really am. Since I was little, I could talk to Spirit and loved ones on the other side. That was normal. I didn't question it. I would hear things, feel things, and know things. I didn't realize how rare it was.

After losing my dad, I wanted more. I needed to connect with him specifically. I wanted answers, comfort. Our family was different now. There was a hole nothing could fill, and that changed everything.

I leaned more into my abilities. I meditated. I paid attention. And the more I reached out, the more Spirit reached back. My connection grew stronger every day. I felt my dad helping me from the other side. I felt him guiding mc. It wasn't imagination, it was real.

My guides were there too. Knowing they were helping me brought so much comfort. They never left. They told me I had a higher purpose.

I always talked to my grandparents in Spirit, but talking to my dad was different. It gave me strength. It helped me breathe again.

As time went on, the grief didn't let up. I asked him for signs. I would sit outside, tears streaming, and whisper, "Okay, Dad, I know you're here. Please send me a sign." And that's when the cardinals started appearing. One at first, then more. Bright flashes of red in the middle of winter. Every time I saw one, I felt a warmth inside me, a knowing. My dad was reaching out.

I talked to him every day. At night, I prayed he would come to me in a dream. Eventually, he did. Those are visitations. They feel real. He would sit next to me, and we would talk. Those visits meant everything.

This was the beginning of my spiritual awakening. I took more classes, meditated more, and my ability to connect grew stronger. My dad was teaching me from Spirit. I felt supported, guided, not alone.

Knowing my guides were with me helped. They reminded me I had a purpose: to help others, using everything I had learned and lived through.

I became a certified psychic medium. I met extraordinary people who became family to me. My abilities continued to grow—I could see, feel, and hear Spirit more clearly than ever. I knew when something was off. I could read people's eyes. I could tell when someone wasn't telling the truth.

Then came the breakthrough. During a reading, my dad came through stronger than ever. His guidance was clear. And he wasn't alone. I felt Archangel Michael—powerful, protective. Archangel Raphael—gentle and healing. The Ascended Masters. The Blessed Mother—surrounding everything with unconditional love.

Together, they became my spiritual team.

My grief softened into purpose. My pain transformed into wisdom. I became who I was meant to be.

Every reading I give, I feel them: my dad, the Archangels, the Blessed Mother, the Ascended Masters. This journey didn't just change my life; it became my life. Love doesn't end. Connection doesn't end. Purpose doesn't end. They only deepen. My dad walks with me every day. And neither are you alone. Your loved ones are not gone. They've simply changed the way they exist in your life.

Grief may break you open, but through those cracks, light enters.

I found my strength through loss. My purpose through pain. My calling through love between this world and the next.

This is my breakthrough.

CHAPTER 11

It Wasn't Supposed to End This Way, Or Was It?

by Connie Love

Connie Love

Connie Love is an Intuitive Motivational Mentor and healing professional devoted to helping people reconnect with their body, their inner wisdom, and their ability to begin again. Her path weaves together movement and fitness, teaching, massage therapy, and spiritual development, shaped by decades of studying how stress, grief, and life change live in the body.

For more than 40 years, Connie has been in the health and body industry. She taught massage and mentored students for 25 years with a style that is practical, grounded, and deeply compassionate. She believes real healing is not about fixing yourself, it is about listening to what is true and responding with care. Her work honors both the physical body and the unseen layers of energy and intuition that guide us.

Now based in Florida, Connie continues to support clients and community through one-on-one sessions, classes, and gentle, truth-telling guidance. She is especially passionate about helping people who feel overwhelmed or lost so they can start to return to themselves with steadiness and hope.

She is known for warm humor, calm presence, and making people feel safe enough to change today.

Connie's writing is rooted in lived experience and the belief that the universe prepares us in ways we may not understand until later. Transformation, to her, is a lifelong unfolding.

IT WASN'T SUPPOSED TO END THIS WAY, OR WAS IT?

BY CONNIE LOVE

I believe the blueprint for my current transformation was set in motion in June of 1979, the month I married the man I will call William. We were inexperienced back then, and we stepped into marriage hoping love would be enough.

After a time, we discovered the dreams and goals we held did not complement each other in a way that could move us forward. We tried, but something essential was missing. We chose to go our separate ways to find out who we were, or who we could be. We wished each other well and marched on. Over the years, I thought of him often and prayed he found peace and happiness.

Life took us in many directions. His included a second marriage with three stepchildren. Mine became a push toward what spoke to me most: movement, teaching, massage therapy, and my spirituality. I delved into energy and could not get enough. Over time, I learned how to combine what I loved, and I concluded that healing was my calling.

Even with all of that, I never forgot William. I knew I still had love for him. From time to time, I searched the internet to see where life had taken him.

Then something changed. I began having disturbing dreams about him. In the dreams, he was drowning, sinking, reaching, unable to find solid ground. I would wake up with urgency in my chest, like my spirit was sounding an alarm. The dreams carried weight, and I could not dismiss them.

In 2017, I came upon an email address for him. I debated for a while. What if this opens a door I cannot close? Then a quieter truth rose up: what do I have to lose? I sent the email, and two days later I received a response. I was elated, and also scared of the unknown. He was living on the East Coast and was divorced. Hearing his voice again felt familiar, and our conversation flowed with ease.

As we spoke more, the dreams began to make sense. William was a good-hearted man. He gave more than was asked and wanted peace more than conflict. From what he shared, and from what I witnessed as we reconnected, he felt used and emotionally worn down. Financially, he felt overwhelmed. He described feeling trapped, like he did not know how to escape the prison he believed he was in. In essence, he was drowning, and my dreams were showing me the truth before my mind could name it.

This chapter is not a therapy session, so I will spare you the details of our lives over the past thirty-some years. What matters is that in 2018, we decided to put our lives back together and create a new one. It was not without problems and complications, but we were both at an age where we wanted someone in our lives, someone to share ordinary days with. He retired and moved from the East Coast to my home in Chicago. We started to really dislike the winters in Chicago, and moved to Florida to begin again.

Soon after, his brother and sister-in-law said something that has stayed with me: if it had not been for me, he would have died before we ever found each other again. I do not share that for drama. I share it because it framed our reunion as more than romance. It felt like timing, mercy, and a second chance.

My picture of our future was simple. We would live in sunny Florida, build a peaceful rhythm, and grow older with the comfort of companionship. In 2024, William developed bronchitis issues, but it did not seem serious, and he was receiving medical treatment.

Then came September 30, 2024. We played golf that morning, went about our day, and in the evening he complained of shortness of breath. By then, I was pretty intuitive, and I did not like what I felt. I called emergency services, and three hours later, William began his transition to the spirit world.

I felt numbness and grief, and then the waves of anger, fear, and disbelief. But most of all, I kept returning to one thought: it wasn't supposed to end this way. Since that night, life has been lonely, challenging, and confusing.

And yet, if I am honest, the universe had been preparing me. While we were in Florida, I had dreams of William leaving me. In the dreams, there was a quiet finality, like a door closing softly. I did not want to believe it. Now I wonder if those dreams were not meant to scare me, but to steady me, the way spirit sometimes gives us a few moments of rehearsal before a life-changing goodbye.

I have reflected deeply and sought answers from the universe, from spirit, from angels, and from guides. The message that has come back to me is steady and clear: my life goes on. My purpose has not changed. I am still called to be a healer, a messenger, and a teacher.

So here I am in yet another transformation, one I did not choose, but one I must live through. In 2018, my transformation was to build a life with William. In 2024, my transformation became learning how to go it alone again, while continuing to grow and keeping my heart open without losing myself. My blueprint for transformation is still processing, and I will follow where the universe takes me.

I am surrounded by friends, supported by community, and held by people who love me. I also believe William will continue to be part of my transformation. In a mysterious way, I feel we started this together, and the universe will complete what it began in and through us.

Do you feel like you have lost touch with who you are, or with who you once were? If so, maybe your own transformation is calling you too, not to punish you, but to guide you home.

CHAPTER 12

The Extraordinary Joy of Now

by Janie MacMillan

Janie MacMillan

Janie MacMillan is an author, speaker, and teacher whose work helps others connect more deeply with their inner wisdom and to live with greater clarity, courage, and joy.

Drawing from more than a decade of guiding clients and students in the Akashic Records, Janie brings soul-level insight into everyday life—making the spiritual tangible and the profound practical.

She is the author of *The Akashic Records Speak: Yes! There IS More to Life*, a book channeled directly from the Records that shares their loving guidance and the story of how connecting with their wisdom transformed her life.

Adventure shapes Janie's life both outwardly and inwardly. She treasures the journeys that have carried her across many parts of the world. Whether kissing the Blarney Stone, crossing the Arctic Circle, or taking a leap of faith while bungee jumping, parachuting, and zip-lining, she embraces adventure and honors her soul's quest for exploration and expansion.

To connect, learn more, or explore her offerings, visit **janiemac.com**.

THE EXTRAORDINARY JOY OF NOW

BY JANIE MACMILLAN

The three-hour drive to Mt. Shasta began with excitement. I'd heard the mountain was a place of expansive energy and spiritual awakening. But as the road stretched on, a heavy thought settled. I recognized that I would never live in a place I loved while my mother was alive.

Five years earlier, after my father passed, I moved back to Ohio from Florida to be near my mother. Florida never felt like my forever home—but neither does Ohio.

My dream is to live somewhere the air feels full of energy. Somewhere with a strong sense of community, where being outdoors is part of everyday life. I picture trails to explore, wildlife and wildflowers, and winters with snow and skiing—somewhere I feel happy and alive.

Still, I couldn't ignore how important it was for me to be near my mother. I wanted to share real, everyday moments—not just holidays or planned visits. It goes beyond the mother-daughter bond. She is one of the few people who truly knows me—my heart, my history, my quirks. We've shared adventures and memories. She sees me, and she is my home.

We talk on the phone most days, but spending time with her in person means a great deal to me. I genuinely enjoy her company. This left me with a painful choice: stay close enough to share everyday moments with her or move to a place I love.

It felt like a problem with no solution. Deep down, I knew that I would always choose to be near my mother, even if it meant letting go of my dream. The truth hit hard, and I broke down in tears, wondering why I couldn't have both.

I didn't know it then, but the pain and grief I experienced in that moment eventually led to a shift within me. Gradually, my perceived limitations and sense of resigned sacrifice began to lose their hold.

Surprisingly, it was during that same trip that a new idea began to form. Maybe nothing outside me needed to change. Maybe what needed to change was me. I started to look at my life differently, and only later did I realize that my horse, Max, and my mother would help me learn how to live that change.

Like my mother, Max was in his later years. For twenty-three years, our relationship had been simple: I groomed him, I rode him, and I cared for him. But something shifted. I began to see him as a wise companion—a teacher, a mirror, a guide—who had so much more to offer me. This shift in how I saw him led me to change my perspective on everything else, as well. I began noticing things to appreciate rather than only seeing what felt like limitations.

It didn't happen all at once, but it was a turning point. I began to value every day I still had with my mother and with Max, instead of focusing on the *not yet* of where I wanted to live. The pressure to move away from Ohio disappeared. In fact, something unexpected happened: I found myself feeling grateful for the prospect of staying in Ohio for many years, because it meant more time with these two beings I loved. It wasn't giving up. It was realizing what really mattered.

As my perspective changed, so did my life. Ohio no longer felt like a cage. I started building a life there, not because I had to, but because I wanted to. I began to appreciate my life—no longer rushing toward the *next*, but enjoying every moment, eager to see what each day might bring.

Some of my happiest moments came from simple routines. I especially loved visiting Max on cold winter evenings. The crisp air, the comforting scent of the barn, a blend of hay, leather, grain, and horse, and the familiar music all around me—the rustle of shavings, the rhythmic breathing, the soft, steady sound of horses contentedly chewing, the rattle of a shifting bucket—felt comforting and grounding. It was my heaven on Earth.

Inside those barn walls, the world felt different. Stress and restless thoughts about what was missing disappeared the moment I stepped inside. Time slowed. Max greeted me with eager anticipation, pawing the shavings and bobbing his head impatiently, hardly able to contain himself as he waited for treats. His joy was infectious, simple, and pure, bringing me back to the present moment. Nothing else mattered. I felt fully alive.

In those moments, there was no pressure to be anywhere else, no striving to be anyone else. My focus was entirely on him. The rest of the world fell away, and I felt a peace I rarely found anywhere else.

I loved being there with him—his steady presence and the wordless connection between us. As my perspective shifted, something in me softened, and I came alive again. I was no longer waiting for life to begin somewhere else; I was living it fully, right there in the glow of the barn light—in its simplicity, inviting me to fall in love with my life all over again.

On the drive home, I always called my mother to tell her about my visit with Max and to hear about her day. Even the night sky felt magical on those drives—full of stars stretching from horizon to horizon. There was something comforting about knowing that both Max and my mom were tucked in and safe for the night. In those moments, life felt complete.

During one of those calls, my mother made an offhand remark that further added to my joy: "Did you hug your horse today?" From then on, I began and ended each visit with Max in an embrace. I wrapped my arms around his warm neck so that our hearts were aligned, and I would linger there, feeling his steady energy—especially welcome on chilly nights. Those hugs were more than a simple gesture of affection. They were an exchange of trust, compassion, appreciation, and pure, unconditional love—a silent affirmation of the bond I had chosen to deepen, and a reminder to slow down and appreciate the love right in front of me.

Looking back on that trip to Mt. Shasta, I see how what I perceived as a challenge became a powerful lesson about the transformative power of perspective and presence. What once felt like being stuck became an invitation to appreciate my life exactly as it was. Letting go of old beliefs made room for a more authentic, grateful way of living.

And yes, I'm having a lot more fun.

I learned that life isn't waiting somewhere else; it's happening right now in the ordinary moments we often overlook. It's simply waiting to be noticed, sometimes cherished, and always embraced. When I finally understood that, I found joy in my life as it is, and a sense of alignment, acceptance, and gratitude. Not the joy that comes from a perfect life, but the joy that comes when you can see the beauty in the present. It was an awakening to what it means to live fully in the moment. The long-held *not yet* had blossomed into a vibrant, wholehearted *now*.

We may all have our own versions of *not yet*—the dream we believe we must wait for. But sometimes the limits we face lead us to grow in ways we never expected. Being present doesn't erase longing, but it can transform it into appreciation for what's already here.

What might we discover if we stopped waiting for someday and opened our hearts to the life happening right now?

What might we notice if we stopped treating the present like a pause, and saw it as the life we have—imperfect and yet meaningful, each day unique and not to be missed?

To live fully in each moment is to say yes to life.

CHAPTER 13

The Learning Journey Never Ends

by Sarah Merlin

Sarah Merlin

Sarah Merlin is a retired police officer living in the United Kingdom (UK). Following retirement, she returned to higher education, achieving a first-class BSc (Hons) in Forensic Psychology, and is currently studying for an MSc in Health Psychology. Sarah is looking forward to a *new* career, where she can use her professional and personal life experience, together with her extensive skill set, to help patients within the UK National Health Service (NHS) and clients in private health settings.

THE LEARNING JOURNEY NEVER ENDS

BY SARAH MERLIN

At eleven years old, I stood on the stage of my primary school assembly hall, clutching a certificate that read *Best All-Rounder*. It was a proud moment, yet it carried an unintended weight. I wasn't the best at anything, just mediocre at everything. That label followed me through my teenage years like a shadow, whispering that I was destined for mediocrity. Deep down, I longed to go to university, but the voice of doubt was louder: "You're not good enough." So, I shelved that dream and stepped into the rhythm of work and life. Thirty-one years passed. The could've, should've, would've conundrum lingered like an echo in the back of my mind.

The Pause That Changed Everything

Then came medical retirement—a sudden, jarring halt. Overnight, my identity fractured. No job, no routine, no purpose. I found myself in an abyss, asking the question that would redefine my life: *What next?* I could have surrendered to the pain—both physical and emotional—but something inside me rebelled. I refused to let the rest of my life be viewed through a lens of regret and a bottle of painkillers. I needed a challenge, a focus, a future.

That's when I decided to go back to school. It wasn't easy. Chronic pain and depressive episodes were constant companions, but so was determination. Over eight years, I chipped away at my ambition and emerged with a first-class BSc (Hons) in Forensic Psychology—at age 56. That piece of paper wasn't just a degree; it was a declaration. Achievement, I discovered, is not about the cap and gown. It's about reclaiming your confidence, rediscovering your strength, and proving to yourself that you are capable—even when life tells you otherwise.

The Power of Lifelong Learning

Education is often portrayed as a journey with a clear destination: graduation. But what I learned is that the journey never truly ends. Each milestone opens a door to another. After completing my degree, I asked myself: *Could I possibly achieve a Master's degree?* Today, as I write this, I am in the third year of my MSc in Health Psychology, working on my dissertation and preparing for graduation in Autumn 2026. Yes, I can. Yes, I have.

This journey taught me that transformation is not a single event—it's a continuum. The learning journey never ends. It is the thread that stitches together resilience, growth, and self-belief. Every lecture, every assignment, every late-night study session was a step toward rediscovering who I was—and who I could become.

Lessons Beyond the Classroom

What surprised me most was that the greatest lessons weren't in textbooks. They were in perseverance, patience, and self-compassion. Managing chronic pain while studying taught me the art of pacing—not just physically, but mentally. There were days when the weight of depression made even opening a laptop feel impossible. On those days, I learned that progress isn't always measured in pages read or essays written. Sometimes, it's measured in the courage to keep going.

I also discovered the importance of community. Returning to academia after decades away was daunting, but I found support in peers and mentors who believed in me when I struggled to believe in myself. Their encouragement reminded me that learning is not a solitary pursuit—it thrives in connection. I am also thankful and grateful for my incredibly supportive family and close friends.

Redefining Achievement

For years, I thought achievement was about external validation—a certificate, a title, a job. But standing at my graduation ceremony, wearing that funny square cap and tassel, I realized achievement is deeply personal. It's about reclaiming agency over your life. It's about proving to yourself that limitations, whether imposed by circumstance or self-doubt, can be dismantled.

Education gave me more than knowledge. It gave me well-being, purpose, and a renewed sense of identity. It reignited a fire that had dimmed under years of ill health and uncertainty. And that fire continues to burn, fuelling my pursuit of new goals and dreams.

From Regret to Renewal

The could've, should've, would've mindset is a thief. It steals joy from the present and blinds us to possibility. For decades, I lived under its shadow, wondering what might have been. But here's what I've learned: it's never too late to rewrite your story. Transformation begins the moment you decide to step out of the shade of limitation and into the light of possibility.

Assign the used-to-be to the trash can. Ditch the should've, could've, would've of the past. Grab the here and now. Embrace the new you, version 2.0. Reignite the fire of dreams and let it illuminate a future filled with balance, positivity, and endless opportunities. I am now stepping forward with greater confidence, expanded awareness of my inner strength, and a dogged determination to fly over fear and soar above self-doubt!

A Message to the Reader

If you're standing at a crossroads, wondering if it's too late, let me assure you: it isn't. Whether your dream is academic, creative, or personal, the learning journey never ends. It's not about age, circumstance, or perfection. It's about curiosity, courage, and the willingness to begin again.

Start small. Take one step. Enroll in that course. Pick up that book. Ask that question. Each step will lead to another, and before you know it, you'll look back and marvel at how far you've come.

Transformation is possible. Renewal is possible. And it begins with a simple truth: the learning journey never ends.

CHAPTER 14

The Tower Must Fall

by Andrea Miller

Andrea Miller

Andrea reunited with her husband, and they live in the Adirondacks of New York State with their youngest son, two dogs, and four cats. She finds joy in gourmet cooking, gardening, and spending time with family. A large part of her heart lives in San Diego, California, where she spends time visiting another one of her sons and his family. Her favorite daily affirmation is "*Life is beautiful if you make it so.*" (Elias Patras)

THE TOWER MUST FALL

BY ANDREA MILLER

Late April sun streamed through my kitchen window, but its warmth didn't reach me. Fifteen years of therapy hadn't prepared me for this moment. I sat on the floor, sobbing hysterically, and experienced the destruction of self. The tower card had visited me with all the devastation it belies. Six weeks in the spring of 2022 had changed my life.

My father was a quiet man. Perhaps not always a good man, but always calm. I have beautiful memories from my childhood; there just weren't enough of them. By the time I became a parent myself, he and my mother had divorced, and I rarely heard from my Dad. He had remarried and "found religion." My siblings and I were part of his sinful past. He had difficulty being around us and being reminded he'd had a life before he was "saved." I spent the entirety of my adult life longing for the father I had known as a child. I didn't feel worthy of his love or attention, and the abandonment ate at me day after day, year after year. Still, there were many times I would sit and cry, "I just want my Dad." On March 11, 2022, he passed. There was no more hope of winning his love or attention. He was gone.

If my father was the calm, my mother was definitely the storm. She was intense and unpredictable. I was terrified of her, though she never raised a hand to me. The unpredictability was the worst. She loved as intensely as she raged, but you never knew which mother was going to make an appearance. As a child, I became an expert on reading her moods. When my older siblings moved out, I was left as the sole recipient of her verbal tirades. As an adult, I realize she likely had some significant mental health issues that went untreated. She remarried twice, each husband worse than the previous. Her third husband was a pedophile who preyed on the young girls in her life. She knew about it, but remained married to him until she passed away. I felt bitterly betrayed. I didn't feel worthy of her love or protection. I certainly didn't feel valued. I hadn't been a priority for either of the two people who were supposed to love me most. On March 25, 2022, my mother passed away from a sudden cardiac event just a couple of weeks after my father. The conflicts would never be resolved. She'd never tell me she'd been wrong. No closure would be coming. With the passing of both parents, literally days apart, I came a little unglued.

I was not easy to live with. Much of my adult life was tolerated, not lived. There was an eight-year marriage to a man who embodied the worst of my parents, a chronic cheater like my father, an emotional tempest like my mother. At the end of my twenties, I left that marriage with three children under six years old. I met a man who allowed me to feel safe. He held me up through suicide attempts and hospitalizations. He raised my three children with me, and we welcomed another child into our family. I was broken, but he stayed and helped hold the pieces together for more than twenty years- until he didn't. He left me almost exactly one month after my mother passed away. To me, it was proof I wasn't worthy. I was unlovable. I wasn't enough, and never had been. So I sat alone in my kitchen, sobbing on the floor.

In Tarot, the Tower card represents sudden, disruptive change. It speaks of upheaval and destruction. Despite the crisis, it is also a card of liberation and reinvention. It signals a clearing of what no longer serves us, creating space for a new reality. My tower had fallen, and I was suddenly aware that I needed a better reality. I was incredibly out of alignment- maybe I had never been in alignment. I had been ignoring my intuition and was disconnected from my true self. The transformation needed to start with my relationship with myself.

As I surveyed the rubble, I also realized I needed to overcome my dysfunctional habit of prolonging negative situations. Focusing on gratitude, practicing mindfulness, positive self-talk, and consciously raising my vibe were key. I began to post positive affirmations around my house like a teenager plastering posters from Teen Beat magazine. Daily journals were written, focusing on even the smallest things that brought a smile to my soul. I made time for activities that brought me joy, and I taught myself to live in the moment. Yesterday is gone, today is important, and tomorrow is none of my business. I started to cheer myself on for every tiny victory. I switched my playlists to happy, upbeat power tunes. I learned that pain has purpose. I accepted the fact that growth is uncomfortable. I connected with a community that was supportive, kind, and struggling through many of the same issues I was. In that community, I heard the idea that just because something isn't perfect doesn't mean it has no value. That changed everything. My life certainly hadn't been perfect; it had been rife with pain, suffering, and trauma. Despite all that, it held value. My relationships with my parents held value. My marriage held value. Even though my life had been painful, it still held value! Realizing that value opened up the ability to embrace grace. I could give grace to my parents for the things that had happened. I could offer my husband grace. More importantly, I could give myself grace. Grace gave me the ability to rise from the ashes like a Phoenix. I no longer just tolerate life- I live each day to the fullest with a grateful heart. And yet, real transformation never really stops- that is the beauty of life. We get to greet each sunrise and look forward to the ideas and experiences that urge us forward.

CHAPTER 15

Skin Deep

by Anne Norris

Anne Norris

Anne Norris is a licensed social worker and award-winning early childhood educator who is passionate about empowering children, adults, and families. Anne uses an empathy and strengths-based approach, utilizing play therapies, nature, mindfulness, and art in her work. Anne is passionate about using authenticity, connection, integrity, and compassion to help children, educators, and families grow using a wide variety of evidence-based practices tailored to meet each individual client's needs. Mother to three amazing adults and one gigantic dog, Anne can frequently be found hiking in nature, hugging trees, playing the piano, singing, reading, planting a garden, creating art and poetry, and meditating.

SKIN DEEP

BY ANNE NORRIS

"I don't think they are happy in this jar."

I look up into the wide brown eyes of a five-year-old boy standing so close I can smell pizza on his breath. In one hand, he holds a laminated photograph of caterpillars devouring bright green leaves. In the other, a plastic cup with a perforated lid, a quarter inch of beige food, tiny bodies inching along the sides.

It is spring, and the butterfly life cycle has taken over our classroom: songs, diagrams, the promise of transformation.

I am stunned. For years, I accepted this ritual without question. But this child has noticed what I never did. The jar is unnatural. No wind. No rain. No sun. No choice.

His words become a pebble in my shoe. When we set them free, will they be different from butterflies raised in the wild? What does the sun feel like for the first time?

No one tells us that transformation is not linear or clean. There is no orchestral swell, no camera crew. Change happens at two in the morning, alone, with tears and a paintbrush, or so quietly you do not notice until your footing has shifted. Some transformations arrive in waves of shame shed within a chosen community. Others come alone, in the dark.

When caterpillars grow, they shed their skin in stages called instars. When those are complete, they form a chrysalis, a self-made, womb-like shelter, enter it as one creature, and exit it as something entirely different. I once believed transformation would work this way. Shed the darkness, emerge radiant.

Instead, I grew up in a house shaped by an angry alcoholic mother whose fear was rooted in her own trauma. Each day was unpredictable. I learned to read the air temperature before opening the door, pausing outside after school to gather myself for whatever mood awaited inside. Children raised in chaos find ways to survive. Some build walls. I built an imaginary world so vivid it sometimes felt more real than my body.

My father worked hard and was often gone. I wanted desperately to please my mother, but her anger and shaming shredded my sense of self. Eventually, I aligned with her against me. I learned to hate the body I lived in. I existed above my eyes, in my head. The girl below became the one we both despised. The body in the mirror was not me. I was called thin-skinned. I was trying to save my skin and survive.

Puberty was a grotesque and unwanted transformation. I lived in constant motion, rarely still, even when resting. When my body was quiet, my mind ran a triathlon. Stillness felt dangerous, not from the outside in, but from the inside out. At ten, my body was in constant spring, changing daily in ways I did not want. I was desperate to push the flesh back down, peel away the extra skin, and find the boy who had lived in my body before. I loved him. He could climb trees, run without covering his chest, and no one stared at anything but his face.

Then, the summer I turned twelve, I got my period. My mother handed me a bulky Kotex pad and left me to figure it out. When I finally stepped outside, stunned and unsteady, she stood on the cabin steps and said, “Well, welcome to womanhood,” then turned back inside. That night, the lake turned blacker than the sky. Stars burned, reflecting like diamonds on the water. A loon cried across the surface. I sat on the dock and let silent tears pool in my lap. Nothing would be the same.

And it was not.

I declared war on my body. My mother and I went on the same diet from the newspaper. If I get small enough, she will love me. Jane Fonda tapes. Hunger. Discipline. At five foot eight, I dropped to 102 pounds. It brought no love. I was drowning. One afternoon, my voice teacher stopped me mid-warmup and asked why I could not catch my breath. I had no words. I just cried. He held me, then made a sandwich. By the end of the lesson, he had convinced me to eat to sing, and that singing was a way into the world. Instar.

I was an average size most of my life, but what I saw was unwanted, unworthy. My body became the place where I enacted everything I could not safely feel. If my emotional home had been a house, it would have been condemned. A cracked foundation, layers built for survival rather than stability.

Have you ever watched a caterpillar form its chrysalis? It takes enormous energy, shaking and wriggling, using its own body to create shelter before becoming something even more fragile and beautiful. Change takes tremendous energy, a willingness to leave behind what feels safe, even if it is keeping you small or hurting you.

More than four decades have passed since that voice lesson. I have danced near the edge of extinction more than once. Survival requires adaptation, not magic. Shame, anger, and grief are stored not only in memory but in cells that need their stories heard and honored.

What first helped me heal my body was motherhood. Each child was a miracle my body accomplished. I felt powerful, and for the first time, I felt proud of my body. With my first son, labor felt endless. When he was placed on my chest, I kissed his salty-sweet head. I found two small dents on his forehead that marked where my body had shaped his. I traced them for weeks until they slowly disappeared. Motherhood gave me strength and the beginning of peace.

I have learned to bring with me the gifts of my past, even the ones that were hard to carry. I am my father's daughter. His laughter, his sharp mind, his kindness. He is the steady beat of our hearts, often quiet, but constant. Love does not pour from him in obvious places. It is groundwater, deeply held, invisible. It will save your life, again and again. I am my mother's daughter: artistic, stubborn, always searching for more—learning to transform the toxic anger, learning to understand the wounds that kept her from love. Her death was what broke the torturous bind between us, setting us both free.

At sixty, I count the days differently now. Grief folds time in on itself, as if gathering yards of fabric for one more quilt. Yesterday, I broke a wine glass while doing the dishes at my father's house. I apologized as I searched for the shards, tears spilling onto the old stone floor. I want to shatter the glass that measures our lives, pour out the sand, and hold today still. Or turn it all back, despite the cost, to hold his hand when mine was still small. Time meant nothing then. He tucked me safely into his arms when he was strong enough to hold me, and time rolled out before us, wave after brilliant blue wave. This time, I will learn to swim underground.

There is no going back. I care for my grief as if it is a small child. We hold hands and feel afraid together, and we listen to music and go for walks. We hug trees, marvel at tiny flowers, drink tea, and watch dust particles drift through the sun-filled rooms. I take it to meetings. We paint and draw. We hug the dog and clean the house. We plant a spring garden and crochet something new. We meditate and pray, lifting our faces to the sun, opening our eyes to meet each day. Over time, grief softens and settles. Grief is as dear to me as joy. Both have stories to tell.

In a recent dream, I am standing in front of myself at eighty. My skin is covered in accusatory words, black ink cut deep and harsh. My older self reaches out and holds my hands. She has sea glass skin, tumbled and luminous, eyes alive and peaceful. She touches my face and says, "*Rewrite the words. It is your choice.*" One by one, the words lift up and off my body, transforming into small white butterflies. One phrase remains, glowing softly on my collarbones. *More than enough.*

Caterpillars become pupae only once. They live as butterflies for weeks, some migrating great distances. We are given an endless supply of instars if we choose them. My transformation has never been about a final form, but about balance within change. Like sea legs. Like riding a bike. Sometimes I wobble, but I find my center. Over time, change has become part of the movement of my life, and less like an unnatural dance. No longer in a jar, I know what it feels like to have the sun on my wings. I am free.

CHAPTER 16

One Box At A Time

by Pandora Pappas

Pandora Pappas

Pandora Pappas is an internationally recognized psychic medium, best-selling author, intuitive life and business coach, sound healer, pet psychic certified crystal healer, meditation teacher and visionary artist. With over three decades of experience, she has helped thousands of beautiful souls worldwide find clarity, healing, and connection with Spirit.

Gifted with clairvoyance and telepathy since childhood, Pandora began reading cards at age eight under the guidance of her mother and grandmother. Of Celtic and Greek heritage, she carries a sacred lineage of intuitive wisdom that she now shares through her readings, coaching, and healing work.

Pandora empowers her clients to trust their intuition, release limiting patterns, and embrace joyful, soul-aligned lives. Her creations include the *Embrace Your Inner Light Oracle Deck, Take Your Power Back Oracle Deck* and the best-selling book *Finding the Missing Piece Inside: A Psychic Shares Her Insight into Having the Relationship of Your Life.*

Through psychic readings, spiritual coaching, sound healing, guided meditations, and energy work, Pandora spports clients in aligning with their highest path and living with purpose, love, and empowerment.

Discover more at www.pandorap.com
Booking & Inquiries: 773-354-6035

ONE BOX AT A TIME

BY PANDORA PAPPAS

There are dates you don't mark on a calendar, but that settle quietly in your bones. March 22, 2003, is one of mine. Even now, when I close my eyes, I can still smell the hospital air and hear the relentless beeping of machines, and the strange clarity that comes when you realize you have become the caretaker, holding hope together for someone you love when everything else feels impossibly fragile.

My mother was lying in a bed surrounded by wires and monitors when the doctor pulled me aside. His voice was calm and clinical as he explained that she had an inoperable aortic dissection. Five percent chance of survival. That was the number he gave me.

I nodded, as if I understood. As if I were made of stone and could carry the weight of this news. Inside, everything blurred. I am her only child. How do you wrap your head around a five percent chance for the person who gave you life?

At the same time, life outside that hospital was still moving, at least on paper. I was under contract on a condo that was set to close on April 15. My son was six, homeschooled, and still needed lessons, snacks, structure, and his mom. My spouse Jim and I were building a bigger life together. It was supposed to be a season of moving up, a new chapter. Instead, it felt like the universe had taken the book and thrown it across the room.

For a few days, everything revolved around my mother. I walked back and forth to the hospital from my old condo because it was close enough that I could. I sat by her bed, watched the rise and fall of her chest, listened to the rustle of nurses moving in and out. At the time, I thought this was the hardest role I would have to play, unaware that an even greater test of strength and resilience was about to unfold. I tried to look steady, to be that strong daughter who has it together, even as my insides shook.

Then, five days later, on March 27, the phone rang again.

Jim suffered a heart attack. He was out in the suburbs at work when it started. Instead of going to the nearest hospital, he drove himself to the hospital near our home. He did that because I don't drive, and he knew if he ended up in a suburban hospital, I'd be stranded, trying to figure out how to get to him. I realized he was protecting me even while his heart betrayed him. He chose the hospital he knew I could walk to, demonstrating a shared determination to care for each other even in the most terrifying moments.

By the time I got there, he was in a room on the same floor as my mother.

So now I had two rooms. Two sets of machines. Two people I loved deeply, lying in beds behind heavy curtains, with their futures written in question marks.

I had quiet, intense conversations with doctors and nurses at the nurses' station. I had to ask them not to mention Jim to my mother, and not to mention my mother to Jim. I didn't want either of them worrying about the other when they were fighting for their own lives.

So, I split myself in two.

I would stand by my mother's bedside, hold her hand, and say, "You're doing great. Just rest. I'm right here." Then I'd walk down the hall, take a breath at the door, and step into Jim's room, saying, "You're going to be okay. I've got you. We're going to get through this." Back and forth. Room to room. Mask to mask.

And then, there was home.

My son still needed breakfast, math, reading, cartoons, and cuddles. He needed some kind of normal. This is where the universe showed its timing like a little light in the middle of all that darkness.

Two days before Jim's heart attack, my best friend had been fired from her job. At first, it felt like just another awful thing happening in a pile of awful things. But because she wasn't working, she was suddenly available. She came and stayed with us. She played with my son, kept his homeschooling gently going, and kept the energy in the house soft and safe.

Because of that, I could walk to the hospital and back every day, back and forth between my two patients, and still come home at night. I could sleep in my own bed, tuck my son in, listen to his little stories, and not have to ship him off to relatives or leave him with a stranger. If she hadn't lost that job, my choices would have looked very different. That's not something I chalk up as a coincidence.

During that month, I did not move through my days like a spiritual superhero. I felt like a robot most of the time. There was no elaborate self-care routine. There was, "Did you eat?" "Did you shower?" "Can you close your eyes for twenty minutes?" My emotions would sneak out in hallways, in bathrooms, in the quiet walk between the hospital and home. Then I'd pull myself back together and keep going.

All the while, that condo closing date sat there on the calendar: April 15.

I can still feel the knot in my stomach when I think about that decision. Do I cancel the contract? Is it irresponsible to move forward when I might be about to lose two people who were part of my emotional and financial support? Was it safer to stay put, or was this move part of a bigger plan I couldn't see yet?

The practical voice in my head was loud. *This is too risky. Back out while you can.*

Underneath that, my intuition whispered, *keep going. One step at a time. This is where you're meant to be.*

In the end, I chose to trust the quieter voice.

The way we moved into that condo became a living metaphor for that season. We didn't hire movers. My partner had seven stents put in his heart, and there was a strict limit on what he could lift. My mother was in no condition to be lifting anything. So, we did it one box at a time.

Literally.

I would pack a box, walk it over from the old condo to the new one, set it down, and walk back for the next. Sometimes, Jim would walk with me and carry something light. Sometimes my son would carry a little bag or a pillow to feel like he was helping. It wasn't glamorous. There was no big moving truck, no friends popping champagne on the floor of an empty living room. Just steps. Box. Steps. Box.

Every box I carried felt like a statement: I don't know what happens next, but I am still moving. I am still building something, even as everything looks like it's falling apart.

On the outside, it might have looked like my life was collapsing. On the inside, something very different was happening. It was as if the universe had slammed on the brakes. For that month, everything that wasn't essential fell away. All the noise, the extra obligations, the busyness—I couldn't keep any of it going. There was only the hospital, home, and the slow migration of cardboard boxes from one space to another.

One month can feel like it eclipses everything. When you're in it, you forget there was a before, and you can't imagine an after. Time stretches and folds in strange ways around crisis. Days feel like weeks. Weeks feel like years. But looking back, I can see it was a concentrated pocket of time where life narrowed my focus so I could get through the hardest part.

And then, almost without warning, things began to speed up again.

My mother, against the odds, survived. She was weakened, fragile, and moving carefully through her days, but she was still here. After we were settled into the new condo, it was time to move her into the place we'd just left. We wanted her closer, in a space we already knew and loved.

And we did that the same way: one box at a time.

She couldn't carry heavy things. She had to be careful, and we were determined to protect her healing. The process repeated itself, another slow-motion relocation. Small bags. Light boxes. Gentle trips. Rest breaks. There was something strangely holy about that second round of moving. It felt like we were stitching a new pattern: our new home, her new home, a little triangle of support within walking distance of the hospital that had held all three of our lives in its hands.

If you looked only at that month on a calendar—March 22 to April 15—you might say, "What a breakdown." And you'd be right. It was a breakdown. Of what I thought safety looked like. Of the illusion that I was in control of everything. Of the idea that my strength only counted if I looked like I had it all together.

But it was also a beginning.

I came out of that period knowing, not just hoping, that I could do hard things one step at a time. I knew that support can show up in strange ways, like a fired friend becoming a full-time anchor, a partner driving himself across town in the middle of a heart attack so I could be with him, a hospital placed within walking distance of not one, but two homes we would live in. I knew that saying yes to a future, even when it doesn't make sense on paper, can sometimes be the lifeline your soul has been reaching for. When did you last leap without evidence you'd land?

Most importantly, I learned that life sometimes slows you down on purpose.

It will take away your ability to multitask, to over-commit, to run in twelve directions at once. It will hand you a crisis so big that the only things you can do are the most essential: breathe, walk, sit with your people, and move one box. And then, when the dust begins to settle, it will give you moments where everything starts to move again—a quickening—new routines, new opportunities, a sense of healing that arrives almost quietly.

If you're reading this and you're in your own eclipse month, I want to offer you a few things I wish someone had sat across from me and said back then:

You don't have to figure out the rest of your life today. You really don't. Shrink your world down to what you can actually hold: the next conversation, the next meal, the next walk down the hall. Let the big decisions sit until the whisper inside you feels clearer than the fear.

Let people show up for you. If a friend suddenly has time, if a neighbor offers help, if someone says, "What do you need?"—tell them. Crisis isn't the time to audition for Most Independent Human. It's time to let the universe use other people as your safety net.

Count the tiny wins. A signed paper. A box unpacked. A full night's sleep. One good laugh with your child. These are not small things. They are markers on the path, proof that you're still moving, even if it doesn't look like much from the outside.

Please, be gentle with yourself about how you cope. Maybe you won't drink enough water, stretch every day, or journal your feelings like a wellness influencer. Maybe you'll cry in stairwells and live on hospital cafeteria coffee. You are still doing the best you can inside something enormous. That is enough.

Looking back now, that month once felt like the whole story. But it wasn't. It was a turning point. A breakdown that cracked me open enough to see what I was made of and what I was meant for. A hallway between who I was and who I was becoming.

And just like those moves, I didn't get there all at once. I got there one box at a time.

CHAPTER 17

Journey Through Loss, Love, and Renewal

by Lisa Randall

Lisa Randall

I was born and raised in Southern California. Married a marine in 1993 and moved to Texas in 1994. Proud wife and mama of two children. I have 3 grand boys all with different disabilities, the youngest is autistic. They are my pride and joy. After leaving the corporate world, I became a stay at home mama until the children got older and I went back to school. I had a successful cosmetology business and specialized in color, curly hair specialist, and eyelash extensions. After 10 years I had to retire, I was diagnosed with Lupus and I had a stroke. I decided to dive deep into my intuition training and healing. I have met some beautiful people I call my soul family. Transformation is beautiful.

JOURNEY THROUGH LOSS, LOVE, AND RENEWAL

BY LISA RANDALL

Early Years and Unseen Guardians

My earliest memories of encountering spirits go back to when I was just five years old. As an only child, my mother often assumed I was in my room talking to my stuffed animals or toy horses. What she didn't realize was that I was conversing with a spirit—someone whose identity would later become clear: my grandmother.

Growing Up and Family Foundations

Being an only child meant I had to mature quickly. My upbringing was deeply influenced by my Italian Catholic and Irish heritage. My mother was one of three siblings, and her life was forever changed when her own mother died at just seventeen. Thrust into the role of caretaker, she helped her father raise her younger siblings—a burden that must have been unimaginably challenging. This experience shaped her into a strong woman whom I admired greatly, despite the complexities in our relationship.

Mother-Daughter Dynamics

During my teenage years, my relationship with my mother was often strained and filled with arguments. I frequently struggled with feelings of inadequacy, always believing I was not good enough in her eyes. She pushed me to work harder and wanted me to emulate her strength. It wasn't until much later in life that I understood the deeper reasons behind her expectations and why they mattered so much to her.

A New Beginning in California

My mother spent her early years in Boston, Massachusetts. After losing her mother, her entire Italian family relocated to California, where she eventually met my biological father. One vivid memory from when I was four stands out: sitting on a porch, waiting for my biological father to pick me up. He never arrived. My mother took me out for ice cream instead, and despite the disappointment, we made the best of it. At that age, I didn't realize the feelings of abandonment and anger that would surface later in life. I never saw him again until I found him in my thirties.

In 1983, tragedy struck again when my mom's sister, my godmother, passed away from Lupus. She was lively and funny, and I cherished our time together. After visiting her in the hospital, I sensed it would be the last time I saw her. Early one morning, I was awakened by a kiss and a goodbye, followed by the sound of my mother's tears when the phone rang.

Finding a Father's Love

Around the age of five, my mother met a man who would become the love of her life. They married, and he fully embraced the role of father, teaching me skills like water skiing, fishing, handling firearms, driving, and boating. He became the man I called Daddy.

When I was eleven, he officially adopted me, and I took his last name. That day was a milestone for all of us, my mom, my dad, and I cried tears of joy, even moving the judge who oversaw the adoption.

The Struggle to Be Enough

As I grew older, my anger intensified, and my desire to be enough, especially in my parents' eyes, became stronger. These feelings persisted in adulthood. During this period, I dated a narcissistic man who controlled, degraded, and cheated on me. I believed I could change him, a classic case of being a fixer and a people pleaser. After three difficult years, I finally left him.

Healing and New Beginnings

At twenty-five, I met the love of my life. We got pregnant and married in June 1993. Around this time, I decided to find my biological father. Before doing so, I spoke with my daddy, assuring him that it was not about replacing him but about closing a chapter in my life. I eventually found my biological father, who wanted to meet my husband and me. We arrived at a bar, and there he stood. His friends greeted us warmly, and we sat down together. He told me he often thought of me and showed me a picture he kept. I asked why he left and never came back; he tried to offer excuses. I realized he was an alcoholic, unable to be a father or husband, as alcohol was his true priority. With that realization, I closed the chapter and began to heal, understanding that it wasn't my fault; it was alcohol.

Building My Own Family

Our son was born in January 1994, and later that year, my husband left the Marine Corps. We moved from California to Texas, breaking my parents' hearts by moving so far away. But I knew I wanted to raise my children outside of California. In 1996, we welcomed a baby girl. My parents visited as often as possible, and we made trips to California to spend time with them. Eventually, my parents built a house in Arizona, bringing us closer together, and we visited them frequently.

Loss and Commitment

In January 2013, while in Arizona, my dad was diagnosed with mesothelioma. I stayed for four months, helping my mom care for him. It was difficult to watch his health decline, but we made the most of our time together laughing, talking, and leaving nothing unsaid. On May 23, 2014, my daddy passed away. My daughter and I were there, sleeping in his room as he left us. I made a heartbreaking call to my mom, and we all gathered to say goodbye. Seeing the hurt in my children's eyes broke me more. With his passing, I made a promise to take care of my mom, and I kept it. Each year, my husband and I spend two weeks in Arizona, helping my mom around the house. In return, she always made sure my husband had plenty of beer.

As time went on, I noticed my mom's health declining. Her heart problems worsened, and I grew increasingly concerned. In 2022, I traveled to Arizona frequently, staying for two weeks at a time to care for her during her heart procedures. On October 11, 2023, I received a call from her doctor asking whether to continue life-saving measures. I was devastated. I lost my mom, and my intuition was strong, and I saw my dad waiting for her with a smile and an outstretched hand. I instructed the doctor to end life-saving measures and let her go. I could not be there to hold her hand or say goodbye.

Recent Tragedies and Paths to Healing

Just four months later, in February 2024, my husband's mother called with the devastating news that his sister had been murdered at work—another blow to our family.

For nearly two years, I have been navigating a period of darkness. Life felt stagnant and directionless. In response, I began therapy to address my anger and emptiness, started journaling again, and took up meditation. Spending time in nature, hiking the canyon, and connecting with my animal spirit guides and GUS (God, Universe, Spirit) brought some peace. In my dreams, I have heard my mama apologize, expressing regret and love. Before she passed, she told her friend how much I had done for her, and that my husband and I would always be by her side, which was true, though I wish I could have held her as she left. That, however, was not what she wanted.

Renewal and Looking Ahead

There has been much healing and growth. Though the future remains uncertain, I am confident that it holds amazing things.

CHAPTER 18

Breaking Down to Break Through

by Delora Ritchie

Delora Ritchie

A life-long alchemist of color, and a glittery soul whose purpose revolves around the ever-changing kaleidoscope that surrounds us. Her experience spans from early childhood creativity with crayons and pencils to formal college training in graphic design, followed by more than 25 years of professional work in newspapers and the publishing industry. Her WooWoo studies began over 20 years ago – she has dipped her toe in many, many modalities and feels there is still much to discover in our vibrant world. She is a Certified Color Coach, Certified Akashic Record reader, and more! As an Intuitive Strategic Business Engineer, she offers a range of services: virtual assistant with streamlining and clerical duties; graphic design and marketing; technology support with personalized training; and a compassionate listening ear. As a Color Inspirationalist, she is a creative visionary and a true connoisseur of color in spiritual practice. She focuses her practice, AuraOra, on the frequencies of 'Conscious Connections with Color' to raise the collective vibration by inspiring change in others. Allow her to coach, uplift, and immerse you in color like never before, as you explore what makes you sparkle!

Join her Facebook community by searching for C3: Conscious Connections in Color

And discover more about the world of color and her services by visiting www.DeloraByDesign.com or emailing DeloraByDesign@gmail.com.

BREAKING DOWN TO BREAK THROUGH

BY DELORA RITCHIE

And then...
When the answers are just more questions.

As I sit here in November writing the beginning of my submission, I find myself in the *messy middle* for quite some time. So often we're reminded of the butterfly's saga: a fuzzy caterpillar cocoons in a chrysalis, only to emerge as a beautiful creature that spreads its wings and flies away into the streaming spring sunshine. [Cue the music!]

But the part that is glossed over in this tale is the pupa—the *goo* that is you.

The pain of growing comes from the resistance of releasing, letting go of what no longer serves oneself. We hold fast to it for comfort, believing it defines us, until the moment it quietly doesn't.

I'm experiencing confusion, discomfort, frustration, but also subtle shifts—tiny sparks of insight that hint at what's forming inside. All of this is teaching me to exercise patience with myself. To give myself grace and time to fully complete my process in divine timing. Rushing it is just like microwaving a gourmet meal, not recommended. When I allow myself to resist the process, I softly succumb to the realization that this is also part of my growth.

There are cycles to life, I encourage you to explore your own labels for what resonates with you: maiden–mother–crone, moon transitions, seasons of life, growth stages of a plant, or the wheel of life's phases. Each describes the process of shedding and reforming—the alchemy of metamorphosis.

What happens during the pupa stage?

After the caterpillar has eaten enough and grown, it forms a protective casing called a chrysalis.

Inside the chrysalis, the caterpillar undergoes transmutation, a process in which its body breaks down and reorganizes:

- Many larval tissues dissolve into a nutrient-rich *soup* of cells.
- Specialized groups of cells, called imaginal discs, develop into adult structures: wings, legs, antennae, and other butterfly features.

This stage is mostly inactive externally, but internally, it is a whirlwind of growth, transformation, and cellular reorganization.

Duration:

- The pupa stage can last from a few days to several weeks, depending on the species and environmental conditions.
- Some species even hibernate as pupae during winter, emerging when conditions are favorable.

Symbolism:

- Transformation: The caterpillar cannot become a butterfly without fully letting go of its old form.
- Patience and inner work: Growth often happens unseen, internally, before manifesting externally.
- Potential realized: The pupa stage is the bridge between old limitations and new capabilities.

Comparison to life stages:

- Caterpillar (larva): growth, learning, preparation
- Pupa (chrysalis): reflection, internal transformation, potential
- Butterfly (adult): expression, freedom, maturity, new possibilities

My reflection stage

Now in December, I recognize I am in the state of re-. I've learned to give myself grace by using verbs in the -ing form instead of -ed. I feel limited when I use the past tense, as if I've finished and will never need to repeat that cycle. The simplicity of -ing removes expectations of perfection, because the task is never completed—it is simply still progressing—recognizing, reflecting, reevaluating, recalibrating, reinforcing, and restructuring, while becoming authentically *me.*

I become aware that I'm gestating in the *soup* of my life. I summon memories of encounters, emotions, and treasures: all the people I've met, the conversations I've had, the souvenirs from my travels, the opportunities I lost, the experiences I gained, and the love I've shared.

And then... come the questions:

What is it all for?
What's next?
What am I going to do with it?
What does it mean?
What will happen if I don't?
Where am I meant to be?
How will I get there?
Why am I here?
Who am I?

In the brain of Delora, my voice answers, "That's complicated."

Setting 2025 intentions

My word was Voyage.

At the onset of the year, it seemed romantic. I envisioned a huge steamer ship that would carry me out to open sea—housing me, protecting me, and providing all that I needed for a glorious adventure! [Cue the music once again!] Uh-huh, now let's bring that down to earth.

Voyage: I am the vessel navigating waters—sometimes calm and crystal clear, sometimes crashing waves in the middle of a relentless storm. My objective: *stay afloat.*

Am I sailing to a new location to live out my days, or returning to the same port of call from which I embarked?

Am I merely a passenger aboard a vessel with a charted path shared by many, or the captain of my own craft, steering through uncharted waters toward a destiny of my choosing?

Am I drifting with the tide, tumbling in the waves, and hoping to be washed ashore for survival and for solace?

My inner voice answers: "Yes—and then, have I arrived?"

Again, it's complicated—can I trust the direction of becoming who I'm meant to be if I don't know where I'm headed?

It's not only about the destination; it's also about the journey. Learning to embrace my inner mermaid and dive deep into the murky depths to discover treasure, my true self, and then surfacing to plot my next voyage.

The influence of the Chinese zodiac

2025 was the Year of the Wood Snake, putting a focus on wisdom, intuition, and transformation. The elemental layer combines the snake's intellect with wood's adaptability. This energy invited us to shed what no longer fits.

To slow down. To listen beneath habit and noise.

It revealed where we had been living on autopilot instead of in truth.

This was not a year of rushing change, but of understanding *why* change was necessary.

Growth happened quietly.

Letting go was not an ending—it was preparation.

And then...

2026: The Year of the Fire Horse arrives with movement and momentum, adding the heat of passion and intensity.

Where truth was revealed, now we act.

This is a year of courage and forward motion, of trusting instinct over familiarity, of choosing freedom.

Clarity becomes action.

Confidence grows through movement.

The shedding is done.

And now, we run.

Setting 2026 intentions

My phrase is *Treasure My Adventure.*

As the new year takes hold, I'm renewed with a sense that I have been delivered. I ruminate that I have been gestating in a womb—soft and squishy—floating in fluids, not knowing where I end and where my surroundings begin. Ever so slowly, my form begins to take shape. Not the outline I was before, but something more streamlined, more carefully crafted—engineered for my true purpose in life. As I emerge from my cocoon, this is the next level.

I can breathe deeply and exhale without hesitation. My shoulders are softer; my spine is straighter. I no longer feel as though I'm physically bracing against the onslaught of the winds of change that constantly blow against my body. The breezes now waft from behind, supporting and assisting me in forward movement. *The universe has my back.*

I can sense my path unfurling before me. I see visions of the Scottish Highlands—where my soul and ancestors hail. With twists and turns, it winds around flowing hills—uplifting and full of possibilities. I do not fear the effort of traversing this path. I do not calculate the supplies needed to survive what lies ahead. I lay down the heavy burden that I carry for many old reasons. What I need is contained inside of me, along with faith that I'll manifest the rest... *this or something better.*

I vow to anticipate surprises, to marvel at small miracles, and to envelope my revelations. I gracefully surrender to not knowing the how, where, or when—to firmly anchor to the horizon and trust the next phase of my journey—to treasure my adventure and the *what if.*

CHAPTER 19

"Don't Sit Here."

by Ibis Sardinas

Ibis Sardinas

Ibis is a lifelong seeker, a natural polymath with an insatiable curiosity. With a background in psychology, she has long been drawn to the intersection of human nature, spirituality, and ancestral wisdom rooted in her Cuban heritage, where spiritual and psychic gifts run deep.

Over the years, Ibis has worn many hats: licensed addiction therapist, corporate trainer, business owner, communications and data sales representative, and, most recently, a licensed health insurance consultant delivering corporate presentations across the U.S.

A voracious reader since childhood, she finished the Encyclopedia Britannica by age 13. Ibis continues to explore her creative and spiritual sides through journaling, poetry, and art. She is currently deepening her spiritual gifts while working on the next great thing!

She lives with her beloved two-year-old “giant puppy” that helps her stay grounded. Connect with Ibis at IbisSardinas@gmail.com or on Instagram: IbisIbisibis.

"DON'T SIT HERE."

BY IBIS SARDINAS

A Spiritual Journey of Transformation and Belonging

It was around 1962, likely in the spring. I hadn't been in the United States very long. The afternoon was cool, and I remember the trees, green again after a punishing winter. My mother and I boarded a city bus after a short walk from our home. I was four years old, chatty, and precocious, filling the space with my small, unfiltered observations. My mother kept hushing me, gently at first, then more firmly, telling me not to bother the other passengers.

We found seats on a long bench along the right side of the bus, facing the driver. As I continued talking, speaking Spanish, the only language I knew at the time, I noticed the driver glance at me, then at my mother. It was not a friendly look. It was curious, guarded, and uncomfortable. I didn't understand it then. I couldn't. I was too young to know what kind of world we had entered.

Only years later did I come to recognize that look for what it was, a silent message. '*Don't sit here.*'

At the time, I had no awareness of race, segregation, or social boundaries. I was simply a child using her voice. But that moment, being quieted, watched, and assessed, left an imprint. It was my first encounter with the invisible rules that decide who belongs and who does not.

An Awakening

That bus ride planted a seed. What felt like a small, ordinary moment later revealed itself as a lifelong metaphor. A moment of unconscious defiance, speaking freely, taking up space, followed by an imposed silence. Over time, I came to understand that although we strive for equality, there are moments when *knowing who you are* becomes the most important truth you can hold onto, and sometimes defend.

I would encounter that look again in life. Sometimes subtle, sometimes unmistakable. A look that said, *'you don't belong here.'* And each time, it asked me the same question: '*Will you shrink, or will you stay*'?

Looking back as an adult, it's still hard for me to understand why prejudice exists. I know some people grow up absorbing the false belief that they are superior—or inferior—to others. But that was not how I was raised. I was born in Havana, Cuba, and lived in what was considered an all-white neighborhood. There, my family was simply *who we were*. When I came to the United States, I learned that people were categorized by color, language, and origin, and that those categories came with expectations.

As a child, people often said strange things to me. Why wasn't my hair dark? Why were my eyes light? I was fair, blond, and hazel-eyed, an anomaly to those whose ideas of identity were shaped by narrow stereotypes. I didn't fit neatly into anyone's assumptions.

Grammar school was challenging. I was the only child who spoke Spanish until third grade, when I was assigned to mentor another little Cuban girl named Barbara. She, too, defied expectations: short, curly blond hair, freckles, green eyes. By then, I was already finding my footing in English. My parents had moved into a Ukrainian neighborhood, and Russian became my second language, followed by English. It was an unusual linguistic journey, one that taught me early on how fluid identity can be.

Misjudgment and Redirection

In sixth grade, I was automatically placed in an ESL class. I was bored out of my mind. I finished my assignments quickly, often turning in perfect papers long before the other students. Mr. G, our ESL teacher, noticed. He asked me to help grade tests. He pleaded with my homeroom teacher to move me into the regular classroom. She refused.

Months later, external auditors came to test students' reading and writing abilities. I scored at a tenth-grade level in reading comprehension. Almost overnight, I was moved into a small sophomore-level high school class. I loved it. We read J.D. Salinger. I finally felt intellectually at home.

Why had this happened? Stereotyping. Misjudgment. And as children, we have very little control over the systems that define us.

Navigating Spaces

As an adult, much of my spiritual transformation has unfolded through experiences of exclusion, resistance, and self-discovery. I've spent years reflecting on how we navigate spaces—physical, emotional, spiritual—that quietly tell us, *this isn't for you.*

That first experience of otherness created a kind of spiritual dissonance I've carried with me throughout my life. It taught me to question boundaries. Who creates them? Who enforces them? And why do we accept them without challenge?

That bus seat became symbolic. A place I was technically allowed to occupy, yet subtly discouraged from inhabiting fully. *'Don't sit here. You don't belong.'*

Rejection as a Catalyst

I've been a rebel for as long as I can remember. Tell me I can't do something, and I'll feel an irresistible pull to try, not to prove anyone wrong, but to explore what's possible.

When I was about seven or eight, I was playing with my Barbies and G.I. Joe; they were dating, and another doll named Skip joined the scene to cause some drama. In the midst of that ordinary childhood moment, I had an unexpected realization. It wasn't a voice exactly, but a clear inner knowing that said, "*Life is like a play. You can write it any way you want.*"

At the time, I didn't have language for what that meant. But looking back, I see it as the beginning of my intuitive resistance to constraint. Even when the world tried to assign me a role, based on language, appearance, or expectation, something in me knew I wasn't required to accept it.

Ironically, that same desire to belong sometimes led me to stay in situations longer than I should have. I wanted to fit in, not casually, but desperately. My spirit knew better, but I didn't always listen. When you know, you know. Ask yourself: *When did you stay too long when you already knew it was time to leave?*

So, what does all of this have to do with that child on the bus? Everything.

That was my first lesson in otherness. My first encounter with spiritual dissonance. From that moment on, I would question why certain spaces are deemed off-limits, and who gets to decide. Societal *don't sit here* moments, whether about race, gender, class, or belief, mirror the spiritual barriers we internalize when we doubt our own authenticity.

So, should you stay, or should you go? Are you limiting yourself based on how you look, how you speak, how much you know, or what you earn? Pause. Check in with yourself. Speak your truth, and listen. Don't allow anyone to put you in a box.

For me, immigrating from Cuba to the United States felt like one long *don't sit here.* A kind of spiritual exile that followed me for years. But over time, I learned to build myself anew—through careers, communities, travel, and cultural exploration. Each rejection forced self-reliance. Each closed door invited deeper introspection.

Our challenges may differ, relationships, careers, marriage, divorce, relocation, birth, death, but transformation often arrives disguised as rejection. What feels like loss may be redirection. What feels like exclusion may be an invitation toward a higher purpose.

As the poet Rumi wrote, *"The wound is the place where the light enters you."*

Namaste

CHAPTER 20

Roots And Wings

by Ryanne Saucier

Ryanne Saucier

Ryanne Saucier is a second-generation broadcaster, media, intellectual property and entertainment attorney. She has served as in-house counsel for media companies for over 15 years. She has worked with various artists, musicians, filmmakers, and projects related to the arts and some of the largest media events throughout her career. As a subject-matter expert in her field, she is regularly requested to lecture on the topics of media law, copyright law, and trademark law.

She is the creator and host of a new podcast, *How Do I Do This? with Ryanne.*

She also creates content on Instagram to inspire and encourage women in their careers, personal lives, and for their entrepreneurial businesses. All of the foregoing pales in comparison to her favorite title and responsibilities of being wife to Dan and Mommy to her son and his fur sister Belle.

You connect with her on Instagram @Ryanne_Reimagined and @howdoidothispod

ROOTS AND WINGS

BY RYANNE SAUCIER

There is a quote from *Sweet Home Alabama* about roots and wings that used to feel like a cute Southern sentence you smile at and keep moving. The kind of line you repeat like a little blessing, even if you have not really earned the meaning yet. You know the quotes I'm talking about. You can purchase them at the chain craft store that sits on a framed sign in a hallway, right next to the kind of *art* that says *Gather*.

Then my mom died. Suddenly, it was not just a quote. It was a confrontation. Instantaneously, I was unmoored and uprooted in a way I had never been before.

The idea of *roots* stopped being poetic. It became painfully literal. Roots make your life feel sturdy. Everyone's very existence starts tethered to our mothers through an umbilical cord, rooted to her.

My mother, Sharon Duffie, was not the kind of woman you forget. Not because she demanded attention, but because she had presence. She was a lady, in the full Southern meaning of the word. Not soft. Not passive. Not decorative. A lady with standards and a backbone.

She was an eclectic personality collector. She collected keepsakes that made our home feel like its own character in our life. A refuge. A place where friends did not just visit, they landed. Her door and her table were always open.

She loved *her collections,* as she called them, and there were many. With her numerous place settings of fine china, the quirky cookie jar collection, and sagging bookcases filled with books on American history, her home was curated to her loves. She loved Christmas decorations in a way that felt less like seasonal cheer and more like a personal mission. She loved language. She loved the Bible. She could debate you on the origins of a line in the United States Constitution and then turn around and remind you to write a proper thank-you note. She was equal parts warmth and warning.

And somehow, she did it all with a straight back and a firm belief that people should aspire to do their best. She had zero patience for cruelty, for excuses, and for anyone acting like their life was over because something got hard. She could be equally harsh and loving. But, she loved you forward.

And in that loving me forward, it was difficult to be her first child and the eldest daughter. The expectations of who I should become were never only about what I wanted. They were also about what she believed was best. Even when we disagreed in my younger years, which was often.

Still, she believed deeply in the sacredness of motherhood. It was her highest calling, and motherhood is how we finally landed in a place of peace. Which brings me to the sentence she said for most of my life, one I began to understand as I became a mother myself, but one I did not fully understand until she was gone.

My mom always said she knew she was doing a great job if she worked herself out of a job.

That was her goal. To raise me in such a way that one day I would not need her for every decision and every hard moment. She was not trying to keep me dependent. She was trying to make me capable. It was her job to give me roots.

Manners. Education. Home raisin'. A moral compass. A sense of what is right and what is not. And then, once the roots were in, it would be my job to find my wings. Not just to fly. To soar.

Growing up, I hated it when she said it. It felt cliché. I also hated it because for most of my teenage years, all I wanted to do was fly away from the town where I was bullied, felt less than, and never really found my place. I often thought, Good God, when do the wings appear? I wish I had known that one day life would toss me out of the nest and expect me to figure out how to stay in the air.

I wish I could tell you that when she died, I immediately became a walking inspiration story. I did not. I am not now. She died unexpectedly, quickly in November 2024, and what happened to me was anything but poetic.

It was a shock. It was trying to function while my brain refused to accept reality. It was that eerie feeling of the world continuing like normal while your own world has split open. Grief felt like mentally knowing I am a grown woman with a career and a child and a calendar full of obligations, and still feeling, in my bones, like a little girl who wants her mama.

It is also realizing that THE person who gave you roots is no longer physically here to steady you. And the terrifying part is that I still have to get up, parent, work, and live. Based on my life expectancy, I may live an entire half of my life on this earth without her.

In the first 72 hours after her death, I sat with the sheer irony that in this hard time in my life she would be the only one who could help, and yet that was no longer possible. Then a particular kind of loneliness arrives after the funeral. In the midst, there were details. There was movement and adrenaline. Then, the service ends. The world moves on, and the quiet sets in.

The absence is not loud, but constant. And that is where I found myself asking the question that eventually became the name of my podcast.

How do I do this?

Not as a catchy phrase, but as a genuine, oftentimes desperate question. How do I do motherhood without my mother? How do I do a career that requires competence when grief has made my mind foggy and my heart heavy? How do I do a life that does not include her voice, her opinions, her presence?

I looked for answers. I found plenty of advice, but nothing I truly needed. I certainly did not need a man in a vest with a solid black T-shirt that looks like it was purchased at Baby Gap, telling me to be positive and perhaps walk across burning coals. I did not want someone trying to fix me.

I needed companionship. I needed honesty. I needed a space where I could tell the truth without being rushed toward a conclusion. I needed a kitchen table that felt like home.

So, I built one.

That is what the podcast *How Do I Do This? with Ryanne* became for me. A table. A space where grief and growth could sit down together without one of them being asked to leave. A space where I could be Ryanne, not as an expert with a plan, but as a woman in the middle of her becoming.

And here is the part I did not expect. Creating it helped me breathe again.

Not because it erased my grief or solved anything. But because it gave the grief somewhere to go. It gave my pain language. It gave the inside of my heart a place to land, instead of just ricocheting around my body like a pinball. Less guru with a mic, more vulnerability with no answers.

In the process, I learned that creativity is not just a hobby. Creativity is a nervous system tool. Creativity is what happens when you need to give the pain somewhere to go so it does not swallow you whole.

For me, creativity looked like a microphone and questions. It looked like storytelling, humor, and honesty. It looked like admitting I do not have all the answers and deciding that I do not need them to be useful.

I am not trying to sell anyone a perfect healing method. I am a mom who lost her mom, trying to figure out what it means to live well with the time I have. The more I created, the more I realized something important.

My mom's story did not end with death. It continues in the way I set a table and make people feel welcome. It continues in the standards she gave me. It continues in the way I dig into the roots of why I am the way I am, even the hard parts. Especially the hard parts. For me, grief made me brave enough to look at myself without flinching.

And at the same time, I am learning how to build new wings. Not the wings I thought I needed. Not the wings that take you toward success and shiny milestones. The wings you need when life breaks your heart, and you must keep moving.

Roots and wings.

Maybe that is the entire journey of being parented well? Your mother gives you roots so strong you always know where home is, even when home changes. Then, she releases you to find your wings, not because she is done loving you, but because she loves you enough to let you soar.

Because our story is still being written through me, and how I keep finding air under these new wings. Not a perfect life or a life without pain, but a life that keeps expanding, even after loss. A life that refuses to let love end just because someone is no longer physically here to receive it. Carrying her legacy and soaring, not despite the loss, but because of the loss.

CHAPTER 21

Life Over Leadership

by Ryan Wamser

Ryan Wamser

Dr. Ryan Wamser is a former burned-out school administrator. A teacher by trade, he has served as a high school assistant principal, an elementary principal, an assistant regional superintendent, and a school district superintendent. He is currently the Director of School Improvement for ROE #40 as well as the Director of the Illinois Area 5 Social-Emotional Learning Hub. Ryan is passionate about helping to support teacher and administrator well-being in any way possible to prevent them from going through the same struggles. When not working, Ryan loves spending time with his wife Michelle and their four kids.

LIFE OVER LEADERSHIP

BY RYAN WAMSER

Like many people, the spring of 2020 was an anxiety- and stress-filled time for me—one of uncertainty, overeating, overdrinking, and episodes of depression. I think everyone went through this in their own ways. As a school superintendent, I was forced to shut down our school district in March. Some folks never really left the buildings, making sure students were cared for by coordinating food service and keeping school business going. At first, I allowed very few people in the building. School lunch delivery was primarily handled by me, our amazing elementary principal, and our wonderful school secretary. We even separated from our hard-working head cook like two ships passing in the night. She prepared sack lunches and then left before we arrived to load the van overflowing with food and milk cartons.

I'm sure our teachers weren't happy because I was strict about the stay-at-home order. Unless it was an emergency, I wanted them home. I didn't want to think about what would happen if someone contracted COVID because they were spending time in school going above and beyond, as our teachers always do. The virtual teaching they were thrown into was done remarkably well. I am blessed to have led such an amazing staff. Technology was in place, and apps were used seamlessly (well, as seamless as possible), with daily Zooms happening across the grade levels. I got slammed in early May because being overly cautious also meant saying no to a "drive-through town parade." Even though other schools did, I couldn't justify 50 cars driving through town, congregating to coordinate the start time, and then hundreds of families possibly coming together along the route. Maybe I was wrong, but it's a decision I stood by.

The Breaking Point

The pandemic didn't stop the usual stressors of the job. You still have school board members who dislike your decisions. During this time, we were also trying to coordinate school renovations and a major building addition. Everything was magnified by the other stresses we were all facing. There is no more grace, or not enough grace, in our society. I thought some on my board took pleasure in my pain, but as superintendents, we smile through it all and act like nothing is wrong. We must lead with grace, even when we are not happy. As a school administrator, this is true in a normal year, let alone during a once-in-a-hundred-year pandemic. To say I needed a personal transformation would be an understatement.

The pandemic for me was filled with stress, anxiety, weight gain, and alcohol abuse. Other than that, everything was great—HA! Positively, it caused my wife, kids, and me to grow closer by playing games, doing puzzles, and watching every movie imaginable. We figured out a decent plan to help our kids engage in virtual learning, with us taking turns going into our respective jobs as required. The pandemic reinforced how much I love my wife and kids. I remember how resilient my kids were while I tried not to break down each day. My daily thought was how I couldn't believe these amazing kids actually came from me.

In the midst of all this, my wife and I decided to sell our house and move into the school district where I served so my kids would (eventually) be with me at school, and I could show that every decision impacted not only other people's kids but mine as well. Not that we needed more stress—some studies say moving is the most stressful thing you can do—so let's do it during a pandemic! We moved in the summer, right before school started, and right as the health department encouraged us to start the year at home again in virtual learning.

The stress of bringing my family into the district peaked as I moved boxes into our house and my son explored his new neighborhood, making new friends along the way. Unfortunately, these were the same kids whose parents emailed me, telling me how stupid I was. That I was ruining their children's lives by not bringing them back full-time. I've never been part of a global conspiracy before, but they made sure to tell me I was. It wasn't that my new neighbors cursed my name—it was more the stress of letting my kids enjoy new friends while shielding them from negativity about their dad. After long talks with my wife, I realized I probably didn't make the right decision moving my family into the district. Great timing!

Maybe it's my fault for not separating professional duties from family duties. My new favorite term is work-life harmony. The last six years have made me reconsider what that means. I knew I couldn't compartmentalize school stress and still smile while walking around the neighborhood. Not that I could even walk around my new neighborhood—my physical health was in no position to help my mental health.

When you're holding onto a thread, and it starts to fray, you have to make drastic decisions, or you'll never survive. I knew I could either let outside influences do to me what they did to many colleagues or take control of my health—not just for me but for my family. I finally came to terms that I was living my life to give back to public education that gave so much to me, but to the detriment of my health. I don't say any of this to make anyone feel bad; it was my reality and probably similar to many others.

Family, Faith, and a Hard Truth

My reality is that my dad died when I was in seventh grade. He coached school sports year-round and taught eighth-grade math. He lived, slept, and eventually died in school. He died in the middle of coaching a volleyball game on January 4, 1994. But you know what happened the next day? Through the shock and mourning, the school bell still rang at Belle Valley South School. Students still arrived, and math class continued with a substitute. A new full-time teacher was eventually hired, and those students carried on. My family was honored to have the school gymnasium named after him. I came to grips at a young age that, regardless of his impact, my dad was replaceable at his school. As an adult, I now realize that even if the principal or superintendent dies at their desk, schools won't shut down. I've seen too many colleagues pass away, and you know what happened the next day? The school found their replacement. But you know who never gets a replacement and will never be the same? Their families and their children.

My fellow school superintendent colleague, Greg, told me something that hit me when I said I was going to keep working through health concerns even if it killed me. He was appalled. He said you could work your tail off every day, and maybe at the end of your short life, they'll wheel your lifeless body out of your office. Then maybe they'll hang a plaque in your honor. But you'll still be replaced, and life will go on. Or you could get to know your kids and actually see them grow up. Being a good father is the most important gift you can give. He didn't even realize how much that hit home. Thanks, Greg—your words were something I needed when I truly started to feel like I had no other path.

Choosing Life

This transformation came as I reached my early forties, about the same time my dad left this earth. In fact, he died at the age of 42 when I was 12. My oldest son was 12 when I turned 42. I realized I couldn't keep living like I was on my way out. When you're almost 400 pounds, pre-diabetic, with high blood pressure, taking handfuls of pain killers a day to ease the back and knee pain, that's exactly what was going to happen. So I had to choose: life or death. That's why I left; that's why I walked away from an amazing job in a great district; to commit to being around for my wife and kids. I left on my own terms, and I'm thankful my board of education accepted my resignation without malice.

All I wanted was a sign that I made the right choice—the guilt of abandoning the district ate at me for weeks. Thankfully, God gave me that sign. For well over a year, my wife and I were trying to have another child. In early August 2020, when it still didn't happen, we gave up, right after I quit my job. We realized God was telling us our family was complete. I gave in to my wife and kids and let them get a dog, and we were on our way to a healthier, happier life.

I was struggling with the ramifications of the toughest decision of my life when, in September, my wife woke me early one morning to tell me she was pregnant. I couldn't have asked for a bigger and better sign from God that I made the right decision. Nine months later, I was holding my beautiful daughter, Lucille. She's named after her great-grandmother, who died sooner than she should have, thanks to being confined to a nursing home during the pandemic. I've never taken for granted hugging my daughter when I wasn't able to hug or say goodbye to her namesake.

It was a new journey to get my health turned around and a second lease on life, to become a better father and husband. When I announced my resignation, I told the staff and community I was leaving to make a career change. The embarrassment and guilt of addressing my health struggles was something I didn't want anyone to know. I appreciated all the kind words I received, but I knew I was replaceable and our high-performing district would be fine without me. In fact, that was the least of my worries, which is why my children still attend "my" school and continue to be taught by the BEST teachers. Unfortunately, thanks to starting the year virtually, I never even got to serve as superintendent with my kids in the building together.

Now I don't write any of this to make anyone feel sorry for me. I tell it to help others whose journey is going down the wrong path, and maybe the extreme is the only way to fix it. I am privileged to tell my story thanks to an amazing wife who said, "You quit and do what's best for you and our family, and I'll always support you." I know very few have that privilege financially, and for that, I am blessed beyond words. I truly believe the universe has a transformational plan and a path for us all if we will open ourselves up to listen. My goal now is to help people find that path before it's too late, like it almost was for me.

The New Journey

Here we are years later from walking away from a job I loved, and I have lost well over 100 pounds and counting. People ask, "What did you do?" My answer is simple: anyone can transform their health, but it must be on their own terms. I went from not being able to walk for ten minutes to eventually building up to five-plus miles a day. For me, it was focusing on mindful eating, drinking water like it's my job, and most importantly, taking care of my family. I also did everything I could to change my brain chemistry for the better, including showing gratitude to everyone who supported me along the way, including my mentors and colleagues still fighting for public education. I do that now regularly by hand-writing postcards of gratitude to as many people as possible.

I also tried to take care of everything my wife had been doing over the previous 11 years. Being a stay-at-home dad for a year was the best and most important job I've ever had! I realized how much my wife had been doing to keep our family on track without much help from me. During this time, we pulled my 4-year-old out of daycare, and he and I went on adventures every day. We did weekly visits to the zoo, aquarium, and every park in the metro St. Louis area with a trail or playground. Even though I may have turned him off physical education for life, it was amazing. For some reason, he's no longer a fan of four-mile hikes?!

I have so many memories I'll never forget, even if my then 4-year-old may not remember. But I have a feeling he'll never forget how to get around the Zoo and will forever tell strangers where the lemurs are. And that's what life should be about—enjoying the little things with our family instead of a fancy title and a six-figure salary.

For the first time, I was able to be with my wife on her maternity leave, spending time together and enjoying our life as a complete family. My health is still a priority, my life is on the right path, and God's plan is still in progress. With faith, support, hard work, and love, anything is possible, and I hope to be a shining example for anyone in that same position. Most importantly, I want to be that transformational example for my children for many decades to come.

CHAPTER 22

Paw Prints on My Soul

by Amanda Weed

Amanda Weed

Amanda Weed is a writer of prose and poetry, a palliative care nurse practitioner, and a lifelong animal lover whose work is rooted in presence, compassion, and the power of transformation. Her bond with her soul dog, Touche', became one of her earliest teachers in unconditional love, patience, and spiritual awakening — experiences that continue to shape her understanding of how transformation unfolds in everyday life. Through animals, grief, and lived experience, Amanda explores the ways love transforms us and calls us more fully into our true, authentic selves. amandalweed@gmail.com

PAW PRINTS ON MY SOUL: LESSONS IN STILLNESS FROM THE ONE WHO BARELY SAT STILL

BY AMANDA WEED

En Garde

We stood there,
facing one another,
épées clasped in anticipation—
our journey just beginning.

Armor intact,
but already loosening,
ready to fall away
as trust learned how to breathe.

This was not a fight.
It was a challenge.
An invitation.
An experience unmatched.

Eye to eye,
weight forward,
listening for the smallest signal—
presence sharpening presence.

There would be missteps,
circling, testing,
moments of advance
and moments of retreat.

But never harm.
Only learning.
Only devotion disguised as discipline.

There would never be another *En garde*
without the first Touché.

I've always had animals—fish, birds, turtles, spiders, ferrets, snakes, hamsters, frogs, rabbits, dogs, and even a horse for a short time. They were my sanctuary, a source of comfort in a chaotic, sometimes volatile, and often unpredictable childhood home. I enjoyed their comfort, appreciated their companionship, and found them beautiful. They were steady when nothing else felt steady, present when people were not, and they taught me early that connection didn't require words, only attention. Looking back, I can see how those early bonds quietly prepared me for the kind of love that would one day change me forever.

But it wasn't until my mid-twenties that I truly understood what it meant to be transformed by one extraordinary soul. While in nursing school, I met an instructor who rescued animals and came to know my fascination with the Chinese Shar-Pei breed. One day, she told me about a Shar-Pei puppy at a shelter, waiting for a home.

I hurried to the shelter, and as I turned the corner, there she was, a wrinkly, wiggly little creature with a soft velvet head and eyes that gleamed gold like a lion's. She didn't just have the spirit of a lioness; she carried a regal gaze that seemed to look straight into my soul. In that moment, I knew she was my dog. Our energies connected in a way that felt almost transcendent, as if we recognized each other from a deeper place beyond words, and I knew she had chosen me, too. It felt less like a meeting and more like a quiet *en garde*—a moment of readiness, presence, and mutual recognition.

Her name came with an almost knowing, *Touché the Shar-Pei* (aka Shay). Bringing Touché home marked the beginning of a journey I never could have predicted—one filled with laughter, chaos, and profound transformation. She was a whirlwind of energy and mischief. One day, she managed to open her crate and escape, finding her way to a large box of Valentine's Day candies I had left out. With surprising determination, she unwrapped each piece, leaving a trail of crinkled foil across the floor. She bit into every single chocolate without eating a single one, as if sampling them purely for fun. The floor was covered in tiny bitten chocolates, a perfect display of her playful defiance.

What I didn't understand at the time was that she wasn't just being difficult or mischievous; she was teaching me how to live with openness and flexibility. Where I might have tightened, corrected, or grown frustrated, she invited me to soften. Her chaos was never malicious; it was expressive. Over time, I learned that laughter was often the wiser response, and that joy could exist right alongside disorder. In learning to laugh with her, I learned how to stay open instead of bracing, and how to let love lead instead of control.

She kept me on my toes and filled my life with stories I never knew I'd tell. We stumbled through obedience class, nearly getting thrown out before finally making it through. She learned quickly and loved deeply. She ran joyful circles around the coffee table, leaving track marks in the carpet as if etching her presence into our home. And in one unforgettable moment, she picked up a glass figurine and slammed it onto the coffee table like a toddler throwing a tantrum, just to make a point. She knew when to be wild and when to be gentle, especially when my newborn nephew visited, and she slowed her movements to a tender, almost reverent stillness.

Then there was the time I wasn't paying her quite enough attention. Buried in homework, I ignored her cues until Touché made herself impossible to overlook. She slipped into my closet and chewed up the startup software for my brand-new computer. It was her way of saying, *Pay attention*, and even then, it was impossible not to laugh, despite the aftermath of her rebellion.

When we lived in the country, she would flip upside down beneath the porch, stretching toward a cat lounging just out of reach. She turned the ordinary into the extraordinary. She loved sunbathing, finding any patch of light that crept into the house and stretching out with her legs behind her, as though she had mastered stillness in her own mischievous way.

During quieter times, we found joy in simple moments. Car rides were one of her favorite things. Of course, even then, she had to insert her personality—once jumping out of the car window at an ice-cream shop, causing me to drop our cones and frantically chase her around the block, terrified she might be hit by passing cars.

In her final years, she taught me about quiet courage. When she turned twelve, one of my greatest fears came to fruition when I realized she could no longer urinate. I rushed her to the only veterinarian I had ever trusted, over an hour away, and he confirmed what I already knew. The news was not good. I implored him to place a catheter and keep her overnight. I told him I would pick her up the next day, take her for ice cream, and sing *You Are My Sunshine*, as I had done for twelve years.

But that next day never came.

Around seven o'clock that evening, standing in my living room, I felt a warm whoosh of air move through my entire body. I dropped to my knees, overtaken by uncontrollable sobbing. I knew that soul, and I knew it was leaving me. I didn't need to wait for the six a.m. phone call from the doctor to know my soul dog was gone.

The loss of Touché was one of the most painful experiences of my life. Her death left a void that can never be filled. It took years before I could even look at another dog. I have three now—two of them Shar-Peis. They are cheeky, rambunctious, loving, and obstinate, and I love them with all of my heart. Without the lessons Touché taught me, I wouldn't have the patience or understanding to give them the grace they deserve.

Even after she was gone, her lessons stayed. I noticed them in the way I approached the dogs who came after her, in my patience when routines unraveled, and in my ability to pause before reacting.

I carried her with me into my work, my relationships, and my understanding of presence. She taught me that stillness isn't the absence of movement—it's the ability to remain open, grounded, and loving in the midst of it. That lesson has shaped the way I move through the world, the way I sit with others, and the way I choose presence even when life feels loud.

In the end, Touché changed the way I see not just dogs, but life itself. She taught me to recognize each being as unique, to slow down, and to find joy in simple moments. She taught me to meet chaos with humor instead of anger, to choose laughter where frustration once lived, and to understand that love can be both wild and still. She taught me to feel on a profound spiritual level. Her presence was a gift of transformation, and I will forever be grateful for the paw prints she left on my soul.

Author's Note: *Animals have a way of teaching us what words cannot. This chapter reflects the lessons of presence, humor, and unconditional love my soul dog, Touché, offered simply by being herself—and the profound transformation that followed. Her paw prints remain, not just on my heart, but in the way I move through the world.*

CHAPTER 23

When Strength Looks Like Presence

by Jaime Williams

Jaime Williams

Jaime Williams is a Pacific Northwest-based hairstylist, Health Coach, and Hypnosis practitioner. A mother to twin boys who not only keep her moving but also keep her busy. She finds grounding and inspiration through gardening, beach walks, and nature.

Jaime views writing as a powerful part of healing and transformation. She is passionate about meeting people where they are and supporting them in cultivating inner peace, resilience, and confidence, believing true transformation happens when we align both with ourselves and in how we show up in the world.

Facebook: H3-Home-Health-Happiness
Instagram: H3-home-health-hypnosis
www.studiojadellc.com

WHEN STRENGTH LOOKS LIKE PRESENCE

BY JAIME WILLIAMS

For most of my life, I believed strength meant endurance, pushing past exhaustion and holding everything together without revealing strain. Motherhood changed that. I learned that real strength lies in presence—steadying myself through uncertainty and responding rather than reacting. Presence, not endurance, anchors my children and me even in uncertainty. One example I use is breath work. I practice box breathing: inhale for 4, hold for 4, exhale for 6, hold for 4, then start again.

Motherhood changes you, physically and emotionally. I see my children mirror my habits, which reminds me of the importance of being healthy and grounded. Without that, I can't give them what they need: love, compassion, and empathy. By teaching them about nourishment, rest, and boundaries, I show them that strength often means knowing when to care for yourself. We work together to build our grocery list and dinners for the week, which helps us set boundaries when they aren't happy with a dinner choice.

Our bedtime is set, and our routine is in place. This allows the messy middle to remain messy. In almost nine years, these boys have taught me so much. I learn daily what works and what doesn't. Sometimes I get it right, and sometimes I don't. That is okay too. It gives us a foundation for talking about mistakes, what they look like, and how we handle them. The perfectionist in me has learned to let go. I have released not only control but also the need to have everything be perfect. Years ago, when I started doing hair, I discovered that perfection isn't tangible. Excellence is. I have strived to lead with excellence, even on days when I barely held it together.

I cherish our bedtime conversations. I hold their hands when we go for walks. When I walk in the front door after a long day of work, the boys come running to see me. On my school pickup days, they jump up to hug me, though they are almost big enough now to knock me on my backside. As I stand firmly in my role as a mother, I find myself stepping into another. I watch my parents change and learn what it means to become a caretaker of the people who once cared for me. Life is funny, how the seasons come and go. Things that once felt overwhelming slowly fade, replaced by new lessons and new forms of growth.

My foundation cracked as I watched a parent begin their journey with dementia. I witnessed the ones who picked me up when I fell and came to my aid whenever I needed them. They stood by my side through my children's lives when my husband left. My parents have always been there for me, even into adulthood. We hold many beautiful memories of traveling and relaxing in the sun on the beaches of Hawaii and California. Grief is a funny little thing. Just when you think you have overcome it, it returns and rears its ugly head. I have experienced many forms of grief in my time on this planet. Watching one parent fade while another struggles feels especially unfair and unkind.

One of the biggest challenges I have had to overcome is stress management. I lived in fight-or-flight for almost a decade. My body hummed daily. The slightest noise would make me jump. The toll was enormous. It affected my weight, sleep, blood pressure, and my ability to rest. It also opened the door to new allergies and food sensitivities. My mission became to understand my body. Along the way, I discovered what works for me and what doesn't. I often start my day by checking in with my body. I start at the top of my head, feeling every hair, muscle, and fiber of my being. I move towards the floor, relaxing each part so I can come from a calm place. Then I list five things I am grateful for in my gratitude journal. This helps start my days well and has allowed my stress hormones to slowly decrease.

That mission eventually led me back to hypnotherapy. A friend first introduced me to it before my children were born. It helped me find calm during some of the most difficult seasons of my life. Learning how to lean in and access my inner stillness changed everything. NLP and hypnotherapy teach that all our programming has positive intent. Even our protection patterns are trying to keep us safe. Sometimes that protection looks like weight gain. It guards the body from unwanted attention. I learned that if I could feel protected without carrying the weight, it was a win.

Going within, through trance, meditation, and relaxation, creates the quiet where the mind can gather traction. Simple image shifts make all the difference. Instead of replaying a car accident as if it just happened, the mind learns to focus on the moment after—everyone is safe, and a new car has replaced the old one. That shift creates space for healing and change. It brings a ripple effect that calms the storm and lets light through the clouds.

When the opportunity to become a certified hypnotherapist arose, it felt natural to lean into the training. The benefits for my body were immediate. It calmed the constant internal vibration. I felt a deep sense of grounding. It felt like a breath of fresh air to no longer feel like a tornado.

Instead, I felt like a strong, deep-rooted tree. I could bend and sway in the wind without breaking. As a health coach, it became another tool in my toolbox. As a hairstylist, I offered another way to give clients peace in an ever-stressful world.

Hypnotherapy has helped me be present in moments with my children, parents, friends, and clients, rather than feeling lost on the ever-turning hamster wheel. By quieting the storm, I find strength in calm. Being present is now my work. I embrace softness, pauses, and uncertainty, letting go of traditional notions of strength.

I no longer measure strength by how heavy a load I carry. Instead, I measure it by how deeply I can stay present with my children, parents, and myself. Presence has become my quiet revolution and legacy. This practice of presence, a calm, intentional way of being, is the foundation for how I now guide others. I teach that transformation is not found in force, but in awareness, compassion, and the courage to simply stay. My main message: true strength is being fully present.

I invite you to reflect on your own definition of strength. Consider moments when being fully present made a difference in your life. Perhaps you can try a simple presence practice. Take a few deep breaths daily and notice your surroundings. This small, intentional focus can lead to profound personal growth and richer connections with your loved ones.

CHAPTER 24

Uninvited Partner

by Sharon Wisdom

Sharon Wisdom

Sharon Wisdom has a spirit-led life. As a little girl, she received divine guidance often when out in nature. Living a God-directed life has taken her to missionary work in Africa and spiritual counseling, including many avenues in between.

In her resilience, facing many life challenges, true wisdom is born. It is no accident that her family surname is Wisdom.

Sharon began writing at a young age. Her favorite medium is poetry and prose. She expresses this with beautiful inspiration from her heart and soul. Her often hard-earned wisdom is peppered throughout her writing.

Sharon lives in the Midwest. She is looking forward to publishing a book of her poetry in the near future.

UNINVITED PARTNER

BY SHARON WISDOM

It's been 10 years since my husband took his own life. That was the beginning of my truly understanding what having a breakdown could actually be.

We grew up in the same small town in the Midwest. I was in 7th grade, he was in 9th. From then on, it was he and I. We got married after high school, and I set college aside to support him in finishing his degree. Along the way, we had 2 beautiful children and eventually 3 amazing grandchildren. Our life wasn't picture perfect, but we were happy for the most part.

I had always thought that I was the strong one in our marriage. Now I had to try to figure out how to manage the glaring vacuum of life without him. I took for granted that he was always the one sure constant in my life.

There I was, faced with burying my husband on our 38th wedding anniversary. All of those years building a life together, and suddenly it's over. In the space of 8 years, I had lost my mom, my sister, my dad, and then my husband.

I could barely take one hour at a time, much less one day at a time. The grief was so overwhelming that I barely ate and rarely left the house. The person I used to be no longer existed. Unfortunately, PTSD became my new uninvited partner. PTSD came in like a roar in the background of my mind and emotions. Images of what my husband had done haunted me like a bad horror movie that you can't erase from your mind. It even manifested physically in my body. It's been almost 10 years, and the roar and the movie come a lot less often, but they still makes themselves known without my permission.

As time went by, I had to learn how to live and function on my own. Yes, I had family and friends who were a great comfort and help, but life felt so different and empty. I ended up finding a therapist whom I believe God brought into my life. This was the first step to sorting through all the pain and fear and facing my new reality.

I forced myself to meet new people, I joined groups online, and explored new ways of doing things that I would never have attempted before. My view of the world broadened, and I came to appreciate and enjoy the variety of these new friends and ideas.

Due to the trauma associated with my home, I could no longer live there. I sold everything I had, along with my family farm that I loved. I took that money and bought a new house in a new town that I had never been to or knew anything about. I was searching hard to find a place of peace that was mine, and when I stepped on the property, I knew it was where I was supposed to be.

I knew this was a place of peace and desired to share it with others, and they came! Old and new friends came for bonfires or a sleepover in the gazebo. Some came for quiet, some for conversations. Whether it was for an afternoon or for days, they were welcome, and life and joy came to this new home. God brought the right people at the right time, and it was good. Lots of love and laughter were the perfect recipe for healing parts of this weary soul, and I saw healing happen in the lives of those who came to visit.

Those first few years were fulfilling and healing, and then COVID hit, and it was like the world stopped. It definitely changed. I have several chronic illnesses, so isolation was extremely important but challenging. During that time, I felt cut off from my dream because my dream and purpose have always been people. I thought that when the pandemic was gone, things would go back to the way they were. I was wrong. Everyone has scattered since then, and lives have moved on. The magic this place once had isn't as strong. I find myself opening my heart and my spirit and asking God what's next.

It's funny how quickly the world can change, how fleeting life is, and yet with each day we have a choice. Today, do I carry yesterday's weight and mistakes, or do I look forward and not behind and see possibility and not regret? So yes, I can say I've gone from breakdown to breakthrough, and what I have learned is this. Your life doesn't have to be shattered by a bullet to experience breakdown. Some days it's going to be expired milk when you really want cereal, or the car won't start, and you can't get to where you need to. Yet there will be days of breakthroughs where the sun parts the clouds. It could be something major, something wonderful that changes your life. It could be something so simple as a smile from a child. It could be a scent that brings back a loving memory, and we all know the feeling of hearing that special song at just the right time.

We all go through breakdowns and breakthroughs to varying degrees. Having the freedom to choose. On the day when choosing is too hard, give yourself the grace to not be ok that day. It doesn't define you or own you, even though the darkness whispers lies in your ear. One of my greatest lessons in all of this is that my choice matters, I matter, and it's ok to speak up. Whether that means asking for help or saying no without any guilt. It is not selfish to take care of oneself.

I had spent so much of my life taking care of others and putting their needs first, and for the most part, I didn't mind. Now I'm learning that if I don't take care of myself as a whole, I'm not my best for anyone else. Learning to love myself despite all of my faults has been a tough hurdle. Some days I ace it and some days I don't, but that's ok too.

These days, I'm still searching for direction. Listening for a wise word, watching for things that light me up, always wanting to be led by His voice of love.

CHAPTER 25

Living After Goodbye, Forever My Terry

by Chris Wright

Chris Wright

Chris Wright is a writer, storyteller, and seeker who believes that even life's deepest losses can lead to profound transformation. After experiencing the devastating loss of her husband, Terry, Chris navigated grief, healing, and the courage to reimagine her life. Through love, community, spirituality, and self-discovery, she learned that while life may not follow the plan we expect, it can still unfold into something meaningful and beautiful.

Chris now shares her life with Michael, a partner who brings love, support, and joy to her every day.

LIVING AFTER GOODBYE, FOREVER MY TERRY

BY CHRIS WRIGHT

I was sixteen when Terry and I went on our first date. It was the beginning of summer, 1977. He took me to our county fair, where we rode the Rock-O-Plane. I was terrified as it flipped us upside down in the air, and he reached over and held my hand. Afterward, we walked and talked. The connection between us was almost instant. Later, we went to his house and listened to his albums, laughing and sharing stories about our lives. That night marked the beginning of a love neither of us could have imagined.

Terry was so funny. He made me smile and feel a kind of love I had never known before. We took weekend trips to Nebraska to visit my mom and spent time in the Old Market, walking the cobblestone streets and stopping at Spaghetti Works for lunch. We shopped and bought small gifts for each other. I remember one in particular—a maroon leather coat. It was long, but you could unzip it to make it shorter. I felt like a queen wearing that coat, because it came from him.

Sundays were often spent at state parks, especially in the fall, which quickly became our favorite season. Many times, my brother David and his girlfriend joined us. We laid on blankets, ate too much food, and laughed endlessly. Those were perfect days.

On my seventeenth birthday, Terry gave me a small box. I was sure it held an engagement ring—we had talked so much about our future together. When I opened it, I found a gold ring with my initial on it and felt a moment of disappointment. Little did I know, that ring would become one of my most cherished possessions.

In 1978, Terry broke up with me. He was seven years older than I was, and society, his work, and our families could not accept the age difference. I was devastated. We were so deeply in love—how could this happen? I fell into a depression but had no choice except to continue on.

Occasionally, we would run into each other. Seeing him was incredibly hard. He eventually married and built a happy life raising three daughters Mindy, Missy and Jessie. Knowing that he was happy brought me some peace.

I married and had a son, Ryan. That marriage ended, and I married again. Life was okay, but it never compared to the time I shared with Terry. He was my true soulmate, and I missed him terribly.

In 1998, we reconnected. My greatest regret is that our renewed relationship caused pain to people we loved. But this time, we refused to deny our love. We were grown adults now—the age difference no longer mattered, and neither did what others thought. For the first time, we chose ourselves. I still wore my gold ring with my initial on it. Terry was so excited that I had kept it all those years. It felt like a symbol of a never-ending love between us.

Terry and I married in 2000 in a church ceremony followed by a reception. He sang *"This Guy's in Love"* to me—a moment I will never forget. It was the first time he had sung like that, especially in front of our families. Music was a powerful part of our bond.

Eventually, we bought DJ and karaoke equipment—soundboards, fog machines, everything. My brother Paul built a recording studio in our garage, and Wrightsong Records was born. It became our passion. We played weddings, graduations, town celebrations, school dances, family reunions, and bars. We were busy every Friday and Saturday night. Sometimes on Sundays, we visited senior communities to sing old songs with them. Going around the holidays was especially meaningful—it lifted the spirits of others and filled our own hearts.

After nearly fourteen years, it was time to slow down. We wanted more time with family, and we were getting older. Terry and I never took our love for granted. It felt like a dream. Something you would see in a movie. We knew we were blessed to reconnect. We used to talk about our greatest wish. That was for our children and grandchildren to experience a love like ours.

We had a dream we were beginning to make real in 2014. For years, we had vacationed once or twice annually along Alabama's Gulf Coast. It was our happy place. On August 16, 2014, Terry turned sixty-one. I was fifty-three, almost fifty-four. We celebrated with family and friends, and in October, we took a long vacation to Orange Beach. While there, we met with a realtor to discuss purchasing a beachfront condo. Our plan was to retire in 2015 and spend six months each year by the ocean. We were so excited.

When we returned home, Terry had a few days off while I went back to work. During that time, he picked up some chairs from a coworker of mine. She later called me at work and said he didn't look well. I had noticed on our vacation that he seemed tired and unwell, so I decided to go home and check on him.

When I arrived, Terry was leaning over the kitchen table. He looked at me and said he thought he was having a heart attack. I immediately called 911. He was taken to a hospital in Des Moines, Iowa, where doctors placed six stents later that day. It was terrifying. He spent several days in the hospital, then came home to recover. I returned to work.

That week, Terry tried going back to work but continued to feel unwell. It became a cycle of phone calls to doctors. One finally suggested it might be bronchitis—something Terry often had once a year. He was scheduled to see his cardiologist on Friday for a follow-up appointment.

That appointment never happened.

On Thursday morning, October 30, 2014, Terry suffered a massive heart attack. The love of my life was gone before my eyes. My son Ryan and I tried CPR, but we couldn't save him. At my request, we were taken by ambulance to the emergency room. The doctor tried everything she could, but nothing worked.

Terry's daughters—Mindy, Missy, and Jessie—along with my son and other family/friends, gathered at the hospital. We were all in shock. I truly believed the stents had fixed him and that we had been given another chance at our happy life together. How could this be happening?

The days that followed were painful and blurred together. Planning a funeral was never something I imagined I would have to do. My heart was shattered. We leaned on one another, trying to survive Thanksgiving and Christmas, attempting to make them feel somewhat normal. But nothing would ever be normal again.

This was my breakdown.

I took time off work, unable to imagine focusing on anything. My mom stayed with me for nearly two weeks. Eventually, I had to face the empty house alone. I spent days lying on the couch, crying and begging God to take me home to Terry. I didn't know how to live without him. He was my past, my present, and my future. Now what?

After I had been off work for some time, my supervisor showed up at my door. She was holding a pizza and a bottle of wine. That visit became my turning point. We sat together and talked. What she offered me was incredible understanding and compassion. She told me I could return part-time or full time. I could keep my door closed when needed, and do only what I was able to do. With her support—and that of my coworkers—I went back. Walking through the door was hard, but I was surrounded by love.

Weekends were the worst. Sometimes I wouldn't speak to anyone from Friday night until Monday morning. I was terrified of being alone. My family and friends helped install more locks and better blinds. I adopted a dog named Bo, a border collie who is still with me today and remains the best emotional support I could have asked for.

People checked in often and took me out for meals or drinks. It helped, but everything felt different. I wanted my husband back. This wasn't how my life was supposed to go. We had plans—beautiful plans for a long life together. After spending so many years apart, I wasn't done loving him. But God had other plans.

The days were long, and the nights even longer. The man I kissed goodnight and good morning every day was gone. The man who surprised me with candlelit dinners and recorded love songs was gone. Our retirement dreams became questions of survival—financially and emotionally. Some days, I didn't know if I even wanted to survive.

I fell into a deep depression and experienced suicidal thoughts. My doctor met with me weekly for months. I knew people loved me, but nothing compared to the love Terry and I shared. Ryan came to me day or night whenever I needed him, and there were many nights I called him. At times, I slept with a knife under my pillow.

Eventually, I had to accept the truth: the beautiful smile and twinkle in Terry's eyes now lived in Heaven. He would watch over me instead of sitting beside me.

Desperate to connect with him, I began reaching out to psychics and mediums. Their messages brought comfort, but it was never enough.

In 2015, an old flame named Michael reached out to me on Facebook. We had dated in the seventies, and he knew Terry—but he didn't know Terry had passed. When the topic came up, it stunned him and reopened wounds for me. Michael had a background in counseling, and our conversations quickly became a lifeline. We talked every night. Eventually, we began seeing each other, even though he lived in South Dakota and I was still in Iowa.

We rekindled our relationship and soon began living together. The love Michael and I share saved both of us. His story is his to tell, but together we have built a beautiful life. We travel, stay involved with our children and grandchildren, and spend many evenings playing Yahtzee. Michael and I are grateful for the life we've built together and our love that continues to grow.

This isn't the life I planned—but it is a wonderful one. There is a Plan B, and it is beautiful.

In 2021, I continued my spiritual journey, seeking connection with Terry and other loved ones who had passed. TikTok became a surprising source of community and connection. That's where I met Elias Patras, who became a dear friend. Elias taught me to trust my intuition and release patterns that no longer served me.

I found a community of like-minded people who believe in the spiritual world as I do. I believe our loved ones are still around us, guiding and supporting us, and that one day we will be together again in a world filled with peace and love.

For now, I choose to live in the present. I cherish my life with Michael, our families, and our friends. I continue to grow and try new things—writing chapters for books, going on a cruise, traveling outside the country. Who would have thought I'd become so brave and adventurous? Yet here I am, becoming the best version of myself.

This is my story.

My breakdown to breakthrough.

CHAPTER 26

The Invisible Threads of Your Life

by Janet Zavala

Janet Zavala

Janet Zavala is a certified coach, workshop facilitator, and bestselling author with over 35 years of experience in the corporate environment, including 15 years dedicated to coaching individuals and groups.

A ten-time bestselling author, Janet's first solo book, *The Nature of Transformation*, along with her contributions to ten compilation books, has captivated readers and received critical acclaim.

Driven by a deep passion for empowering professional women and those navigating midlife transitions, Janet specializes in helping individuals cultivate confidence, release limiting beliefs, and embrace their innate strengths to reach new heights of success. Her work guides readers and clients in creating authentic, balanced, and fulfilling lives aligned with their aspirations and values.

Connect with Janet:

Website: JanetZavalaCoaching.com
Email: Janet@JanetZavalaCoaching.com
Substack: Janet the Midlife Feminist @midlifefeminist

THE INVISIBLE THREADS OF YOUR LIFE

BY JANET ZAVALA

The line between a healthy boundary and an unhealthy manifestation of trauma can be hard to distinguish.

The only way to tell them apart is to pull on the threads of life's experiences.

Is there a lesson to learn? Is there healing that needs to happen? What bonds are worth fighting through the protective impulses of early trauma? What relationships are meant to unravel? Which ones are meant to survive?

We avoid the unraveling, hoping for a respectful resolution that may never come.

We stitch together the sweater, creating unfamiliar patterns, hoping to make something whole that was perhaps meant to fall apart.

Or we create something unexpected and beautiful.

Your Memories Are Your Threads

The memory clips that play in your head are clues to the threads you're meant to pull. They remain so you can get a better understanding of life. They stick to you because it could be the source of your current discomfort.

A clip that frequently pops up for me is a scene from my great-uncle's funeral.

Only one memory remains from that day. When the services were over, everyone walked to their cars in the gravelly parking lot at the small country church. The next destination was the cemetery. What happened next erased the memory of every other scene from my first funeral.

As my mom and I approached the family car to travel to the burial site, her sister, already in the car, said to my mom, "You're not welcome here."

Her small but biting statement left us shocked and stranded.

The sadness I remember from that day wasn't the loss of my kindly great uncle. It was the suffocating feeling of rejection.

My mom, never demonstratively sensitive, looked like a deep wound had been reopened as the breath left her body and her face turned red.

A decades-long silence between my mom and aunt stretched before this incident and lasted their lifetimes.

I always thought of it as our family's special form of punishment. Silence was a weapon. Not a boundary.

Early in my life, everyone around me modeled our inherited dysfunction. As a preteen, I felt the sting of the anticipated silence around family.

We were experts in "no contact" before no contact had its name.

Fifteen years later, I would be in the middle of my own make-or-break moment. Step one in my healing process. A family member was scolding me for something undeserving and unreasonable. Anger was their weapon. I knew anger became silence. The pattern I'd witnessed all my life.

Silences erupted and lasted months, years, and stretched into decades. And lifetimes.

I decided that day, if a toxic cycle of behavior changes the person I am in a bad way, if it makes me a sad, angry, miserable person, then I would work to ensure those experiences don't have a place in my life. I would choose silence. Not to punish, but to shield.

I was a mom by then. I needed to show up for my son without the weight of the emotional manipulation I experienced throughout my life.

I was starting to form a picture of how I want to show up with others and the boundaries I need to maintain.

I'm hyperaware of the trauma responses I still carry that make me want to retreat before I experience the agony and confusion of loss again.

The next step in my healing was to ensure the relationships I had were rich and honest. It's a state that's hard to achieve if your fear prevents you from doing the work required to create and maintain them.

I was missing the critical skills I needed to resolve conflict, set healthy boundaries, and the ability to express my feelings without the overwhelming fear of rejection.

I know now my walls often felt like rejection to the people I care about most. My skills of avoidance look like I don't care.

When I do.

A lot.

The more I cared, the more I avoided deep conversations that might lead to them abandoning me.

So, I abandoned them (and myself) first.

Full Circle

Four decades after my great-uncle's funeral, my son and I were sitting on my back patio. I don't remember the source of our tension. The focus for me was about how I show up. I've always had a cautious and fearful approach when the person in front of me could hurt me the most with their silence. It was about my fear and how it prevented me from showing up fully. Silence was my lived experience, not his inheritance.

In the decades that passed, I've had only a handful of relationships I cared enough to push past the terror and likely irrational expectation of being excluded from someone's life.

My emotions welled up in my throat as we talked.

"If you want a relationship with me, you have to make an effort."

I explained to him the origin of my behaviors. I assured him my avoidance was because of my trauma. And I promised to do better. Get better. Try harder.

My avoidance tactic to prevent people from rejecting me ultimately had the same outcome.

I'm a grandma now. I'm focused on not repeating generational patterns. I'm committed to pulling the threads.

I've learned to trust myself because I've become pretty good at setting healthy boundaries. I set them inside relationships. I can tell when it was meant to unravel and fall away from my life.

I'm still not the best at expressing myself. The lump in my throat begins to form. I remind myself that I've pushed past more challenging fears.

I continue to learn. My son is the best at stating his boundaries and holding them. He doesn't get it from me. He teaches me in unexpected ways.

I continually check myself to ensure I'm proactively holding others' boundaries. They deserve my respect.

I moderate my expectations of others. They are not responsible for validating or soothing my fears. That's my job.

Knowledge, growth, and healing are the threads you pull for a lifetime.

www.ingramcontent.com/pod-product-compliance
Lightning Source LLC
LaVergne TN
LVHW020715110826
845149LV00012B/2273

9781971052113